THE ULTIMATE GUIDE TO CARVING INCREDIBLE ERASER STAMPS

Pink Eraser ART

SERENA RIOS MCRAE

Pink Eraser Art:
The Ultimate Guide to Carving Incredible Eraser Stamps

Serena Rios McRae

Project editor: Kelly Reed
Project manager: Lisa Brazieal
Marketing manager: Koryn Olage
Copyeditor: Michelle Drown
Layout: Anthony Paular Design
Cover design: Aren Straiger

ISBN: 979-8-888-143-995

1st Edition (1st printing)

Rocky Nook Inc.
1010 B Street, Suite 350
San Rafael, CA 94901
USA

Represented in the E.U. by:
Rheinwerk Verlag GmbH
Rheinwerkallee 4
53227 Bonn
Germany

service@rheinwerk-verlag.de

www.rockynook.com
info@rockynook.com
(415) 747-8756

Distributed in the UK and Europe by Publishers Group UK
Distributed in the U.S. and all other territories by Publishers Group West

Library of Congress Control Number: 2025934035

Printed in China.

Table of Contents

Chapter 1: What Is Pink Eraser Art? 1

Chapter 2: Pink Eraser Art Supplies 11

Chapter 3: Getting Started: Basic Carving Safety and Knowledge 15

Chapter 4: Border or No Border? 27

Chapter 5: Positive and Negative Space 33

Chapter 6: Transferring Your Design onto an Eraser 41

Chapter 7: Carving Depth 47

Chapter 8: Composition: Framing Your Image 51

Chapter 9: Image Styles 61

Chapter 10: Cutting Clean Lines 69

Chapter 11: Marks and Lines 73

Chapter 12: Spacing Out Letters 85

Chapter 13: Circles, Curves, and Cursive 93

Chapter 14: Carving Those Tiny Details 101

Chapter 15: Creating Drama with Lighting 107

Chapter 16: Drawing and Perspective 117

Chapter 17: Multi-Stamp Sets 129

Chapter 18: All-In-One Stamps 137

Chapter 19: Triptych Prints 143

Chapter 20: Oddly Sized Eraser Art 151
Chapter 21: Using Photographs in Printmaking 155
Chapter 22: Reduction Printing 161
Chapter 23: Sample Fonts for Text 171
Chapter 24: Creating Your Prints 177
Chapter 25: Take it Further 185
Chapter 26: Evolution of the Pink Eraser Art Project 201

Final Thoughts 207
Global Gallery: Eraser Art from Around the World 209
Acknowledgements 217
About the Author 219

1

What Is Pink Eraser Art?

A year ago, if you did an Internet search for pink eraser art you would have been greeted with sketchbook pages full of pencil drawings, acrylic and gouache paintings of pink erasers, or photographs of vintage eraser collections. Sketching the random thing on your desk is a favorite pastime for artists, after all. However, a year after the explosion of the Pink Eraser Art Project movement, you will now find images and videos from artists across the world of pink (and white, blue, green, even rainbow) erasers being cut and carved to create relief prints.

Pink eraser art is the act of using the most overlooked office supply, the pink eraser, as a carving block for the creation of teeny-tiny block prints.

How Did the Pink Eraser Art Project Start?

I enjoy pretending to be committed to the many drawing challenges that take place each October on Instagram, but in 2022 a print-making challenge came on my radar and I was struck with an eagerness to participate. Unfortunately, my husband had been recently hospitalized, and medical bills were stacking up as we jumped through all of the insurance hoops and fought with the hospital. I needed a tactile, creative outlet to regulate my emotions through the trials of that moment, but had zero funding to commit to thirty days of Speedy Carve or linoleum blocks.

I knew in my gut that the physical work of carving daily would be good for me in such a stressful life moment, and as I chatted with Jenna, of @naptimepress on Instagram, she told me, "Yes, I am carving for the printing challenge! I am going to use this box of erasers I have laying around!" And that brilliant moment was the start of an obsession that has carried me through almost two hundred miniature relief carvings. I could not afford slabs of linoleum or branded carving rubber, but I could absolutely afford to purchase a $12 box of erasers! Huge shoutout to Jenna for inspiring me to look outside of the art supply store.

I purchased a box of erasers, dug out my carving blade from the single art class I took in college, and dove into the month-long art challenge. The first carving was

fun. The second carving settled my signature border that I carve around each piece. The third eraser solidified my obsession, and the fourth eraser went immediately viral. By the time I carved the fifth eraser (which I recorded carving while a passenger in our Jeep on a road trip) I had the idea in mind: "This is going to be an entire project, and I am going to carve one hundred erasers."

And so, the Pink Eraser Art Project was born! I started the @PinkEraserArt account on TikTok at the beginning of October 2022 exclusively to record the project and watched my teeny-tiny artworks reach thousands of views and likes within the first week of posting. It was such an experience. I love watching artists break away from the gatekeeping of art galleries by going viral on social media, and I am happy to have had my artwork embraced by the people of the world so quickly.

Starting a Movement

When I started carving miniature artworks into teeny-tiny pink erasers it was fun enough that I had hoped it might be embraced by the Internet, but I did not expect it to become an entire movement! My inbox has been filled day after day with messages from people all over the world thanking me for making the art of carving relief prints feel accessible and affordable. I have received message after message from people who have always wanted to carve or use to carve but let it drop away as they began adulting. Each one of them has told me, "I just needed to thank you for showing me how to get back to what I love. This feels so good."

It is really cool to have discovered something that simplifies an art form for people across the globe. I have discussed with so many people from the USA to Australia to the Netherlands and more about what it could possibly be about carving erasers that removes all intimidation from creating artwork, and I think we figured it out.

Every single one of us has owned a pink eraser or used a pink eraser in class. We have all driven the tips of our pencils into an eraser with the rage of a nine-year-old late to recess. We have all torn our eraser in half during math class or incessantly erased just to blow away the little rubber shreds that are left behind. In short, each and every one of us has already in our life brutally trashed this medium, and so drawing on it, cutting into it, are already things we have done before. And because we have done it before, we know we can do it again.

Blank-Page Anxiety and How the Cost of Tools Blocks Us

As I have shared pink eraser art with artists and hobbyists across the world, there is one comment that is so often made: "This doesn't feel intimidating at all, because I know if I mess up it's no big deal." Think about how often we find ourselves collecting beautiful papers and leather journals crafted by the skilled hands of artisans and we never draw within them. We look at them, we gather them in beautiful displays, we pull them off the shelf to smell them, and then lovingly tuck them back into their space without ever cracking open the pages to create art inside. Why do we do this! There are a few reasons why I have a shrine of empty sketchbooks. The first is that seeking out a beautifully made book is a hobby in itself. The second is that I am holding onto these lovingly crafted items for the perfect project or inspiration. And the third is that I am just afraid to ruin them.

I am not pointing this out to say it is a problem. Craftspeople are inspiring and books are also works of art on their own and collecting them is a joy. I love my sketchbook collection! I have a sketchbook that is a perfect circle when opened, and the cover is naturally dyed with peonies. It takes my breath away. I have a leather-bound sketchbook made with vintage library index cards for pages. It is so romantic. I have a sketchbook bound with a used pizza box and paper bags. Why do I love it so much? I don't know, but it struck me, and I paid dollars to have it. I have a sketchbook that is heavier than all the rest because it is made from rocks and is apparently waterproof and indestructible. I found it in a luxurious stationary shop in Carmel-by-the-Sea, and I could maybe knock someone out with it if I tried. It is not wrong to love things because they are beautiful and made with the love and care of their creators.

Some of these sketchbooks I have collected exist simply to be appreciated. The book that is a circle, dyed with natural colors and botanicals? I know exactly what I want to create inside of her pages, but I am waiting for the right time. I know the time will come when that is exactly the project I want to do, and waiting to be in that headspace is okay with me. One of the earliest sketchbooks I collected in my artistic career I discovered from an artisan I met at a local market, and it is bound with the most striking white leather. I loved this book for two reasons: it is very small, and it is elongated, as if for landscapes. The paper is for watercolors, and I purchased it thinking of watercoloring the beautiful Sonoran Desert where I live. I held

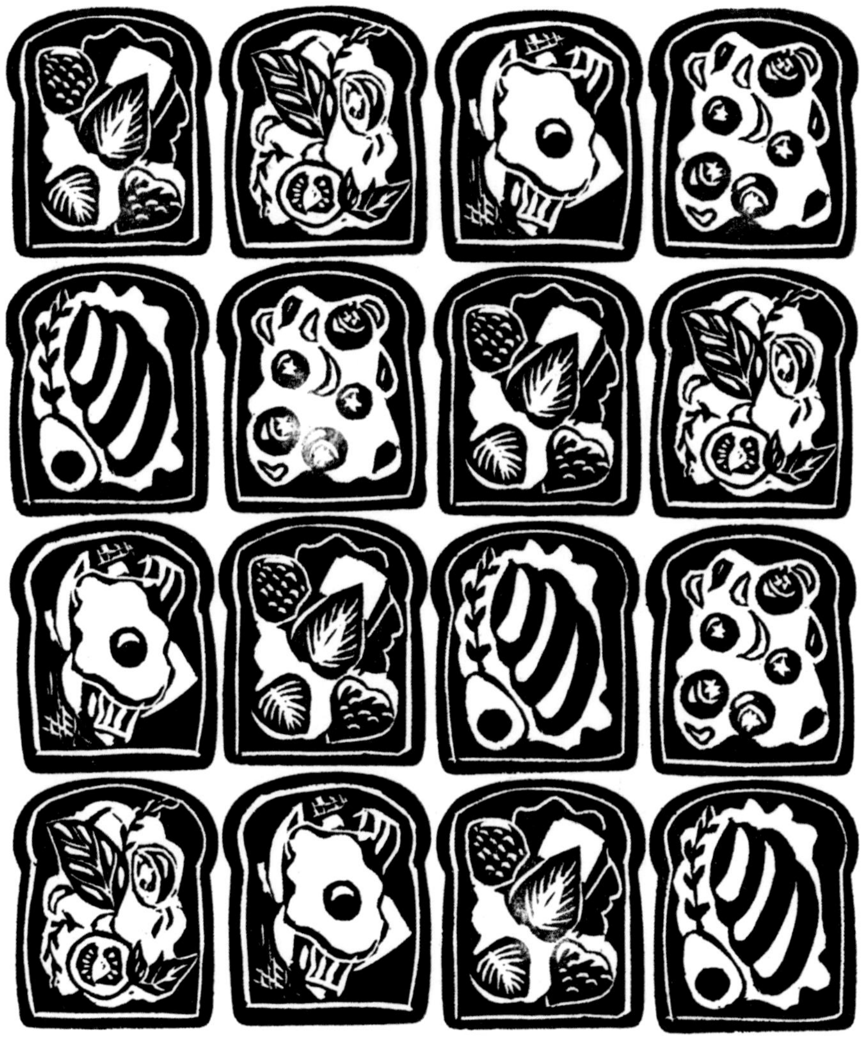

Toasts.
Carved from tiny toast erasers.
Serena Rios McRae of Cactus Clouds Art 2024

onto it for that purpose, until I was met with a new medium, and realized that pink eraser art was actually what that sketchbook had been made for. I had it in my possession for two years before I discovered the perfect project for it, and the day I made the realization I felt the sparkles of fate, and so much joy. Collecting beautiful things and saving lovely materials for the right moment is not bad.

The only thing that makes my heart ache about some of my sketchbook collection is the ugly truth that I also feel a lack of faith in myself to do them justice. I am truly afraid to ruin some of them. The idea that my creativity could ruin something feels so dreary and heavy, and I am still working on healing that part of my mentality. I deserve to create art inside of beautiful sketchbooks. We all deserve to use those beautiful paints we have been saving. We are allowed to open that expensive set of pens. We don't need to wait to be a master at a medium to use the best materials. But until we reach that level of confidence in ourselves, using the less-expensive materials is freeing, healing, and I believe will help us gain that confidence in ourselves that we need to trust our creativity.

And so, not only are pink erasers an affordable (and thus accessible) art medium, but the affordability actually holds the power to create more freely. I believe so many artists experience what we call blank page anxiety, because we do have a lack of faith in our abilities and because of that we are afraid to ruin our materials. It is one thing to imagine a piece inside our mind, and another entirely to create it with our hands for others to see. Add expensive materials to the mix, and it is easy to quit before we have even begun. We see the price tag, and we balk. The answer to this issue is and always has been: lower the amount on the price tag!

Simple sketchbooks exist to work out ideas before we reach for the canvas. And pink erasers exist, now, to learn how to carve, to create daily artwork, to create full collections of artwork, if we wish, without the commitment to spend big dollars to do so. Messing up on a large slab of linoleum could be a mistake that could bring us to tears, but messing up on a little pink eraser that comes in a box of thirty-six is not so consequential. Pink erasers truly do make printmaking less intimidating because the risk to us is low, and when an artistic medium is less intimidating, we are more likely to take the time to try it, and more likely to try again when we fail.

Making Time for Creativity

We are living in a brutal state of being in the world right now. The world is moving faster, and we are constantly connected to an overwhelming amount of people and information. Things are more expensive, and average incomes aren't matching our basic needs. As we struggle to make rent, take on additional jobs, or work as much overtime as possible, our mental and emotional health takes a back seat. We are talking more openly than any generation before us about the importance of self-care and mental wellness, to the point that capitalism has also taken these from us. So, we buy the bath bombs and the self-care guided journals, but then they go into our bedside table drawer and live there, untouched and forgotten.

As a society, we have shunned art and creativity and the importance these things hold for our souls. I work the artisan market scene in my city, and the comment I hear more than anything else from shoppers is, "I use to love doing art when I was a kid." There is a point, and I believe it is shortly after the graduation from high school, that we set creativity to the side, because that is what we are taught we must do to be an adult. Our time becomes more valuable as we begin to depend on ourselves, and so we must choose priorities, and rarely does creativity make the cut.

The second most common comment I hear while working artisan markets is, "I wish I could do that." And I tell every single person who mutters these words at my booth, "You can. You must only give yourself back the time."

I believe that part of the reason the Pink Eraser Art Project has exploded into a global trend is because it is a naturally limited artistic medium. A pink eraser only has so much space to be carved. And so, people try out carving an eraser and realize that they have created an entire work of art in only minutes. Not only is this a gratifying boost of serotonin and dopamine necessary for our minds and emotions to thrive, it also makes us realize that creative time is attainable. We can fit the time for the self-care of creativity into our lives, no matter how busy.

Using This Book

As I research new art forms, I can watch endless videos and read all of the books, but until I put a technique into practice, I simply can't wrap my head around it. In this book, you will find a list of techniques and details that will help you master carving miniature stamps out of erasers. As I teach you each technique, you will see examples of my own eraser carvings, followed by a lesson or prompt for you to put that technique into practice. I urge you not to allow yourself to be too intimidated to jump in and begin. Do not compare your first few erasers to my 190th eraser! I invite you to copy the artwork and ideas in the hands-on lessons onto your own work and then try your own ideas as you practice the techniques.

As you learn from this book and work through the examples, I hope you find the low-stakes nature of the medium calming. I hope you gain the confidence to prioritize creative time in your daily or weekly routine. I hope it affects you in a positive way and buoys you up. Happy carving!

—*Serena*

2

Pink Eraser Art Supplies

Erasers. Rubber or acrylic erasers of many brands have been tested by carvers around the world, and we have yet to find one that is not up to the job. If you have an old, dried-up eraser in the bottom of your backpack, use it! Remember, people have been carving wood blocks longer than linoleum and rubber. A fresh box of erasers will be ready to carve and will feel so nice to cut into, but human beings have been creating art with just about anything for a very long time, so being creative and willing with what is available to you could lead to something amazing or at least can tide you over until your erasers arrive in the mail. And don't feel constricted to use a certain size or shape either. If you find a comically large eraser that makes you laugh out loud, use it! If you want to try to carve the end of a pencil eraser into something absolutely tiny, go for it! If your children have a package of erasers shaped like cartoons or fruit, dive in! There are no rules.

Carving blades. There are two keys to finding the perfect blades for carving erasers. The first is that you need teeny-tiny blades, because you will be carving teeny-tiny surfaces. V-shaped blades are ideal for the smallest details, and being able to swap out for a wider U-shaped blade will help when you have larger areas to carve.

The second is that you want to be able to hold as closely to the blade tip as possible (we'll get into this more later). The best carving blade set that meets these two necessities is the Speedball set with interchangeable blades that can be found at most art and craft stores. It has the smallest V-shaped blade that I have found on the market; is small, allowing for precise movements; and is easily portable for carving on the go.

Ink. Any standard ink pad works great for printing your eraser artwork, but there are some things to take note of. Do you want your ink to be permanent, archival, or washable? I like to make all of my prints with Ranger's Archival Ink Pads. They have the blackest black that I have found. I also prefer to keep a washable ink pad in my to-go carving kit. While carving on the go, in sports bleachers or at a coffee shop, you never know if you're going to drop your ink pad or eraser on your lap or on the furniture, and archival or permanent ink can be an issue here, so washable ink may be preferable in your go bag. You can use printing ink and a brayer with tiny pink erasers, but often my cuts can be so shallow that the printing ink is too thick and fills in the smallest grooves during application. My overall preference is ink pads over roll-on ink. In summary, I love archival ink for making prints, washable ink for carving on the go, and printing ink can be used on bold designs to print on fabric or paper.

Paper. Any paper is good for testing your prints. I love tiny notebooks, especially when they are the perfect size and shape for my erasers. When you pack your to-go bag, don't forget to fold up a paper for testing, and a second one for cleaning the ink off of your eraser before you pack up.

Pencil. A basic number 2 pencil will be your best friend as you learn eraser carving. You can create sketches and transfer them to your eraser with ease when using a softer graphite. You will learn how to transfer sketches onto your surface later in this book.

To-Go Bag. Part of the joy of this medium is the ability to toss it in your bag and take it with you! I use a small leather pouch that fits my carving blades, a few erasers, ink, a tiny notebook, and a pencil. I always store my blades and ink in this bag so that I can grab it as I head out the door if I am itching to work with my hands. I have carved while a passenger on the highway, while watching my kid run laps from the bleachers, while camping, in tropical greenhouses, on the beach, and at the park. It is important to have a closable pouch where you can collect all of your shavings as you work, especially while in nature. Art on the go is awesome and so is packing out our artistic waste.

Bandages. I'm only slightly joking. In actuality it is probably a good idea to have some on hand, especially if you are carving in unusual places or have never carved before. I had never kept bandages with me until I purchased my first set of professional-grade blades, and inside the box was a Band-Aid dispenser. I laughed, felt slightly humbled, and then decided to add them to the list.

Marker. After you finalize your sketch, you can use a marker to color your eraser surface. This will give a contrast to your surface so you can more easily see your cuts and details.

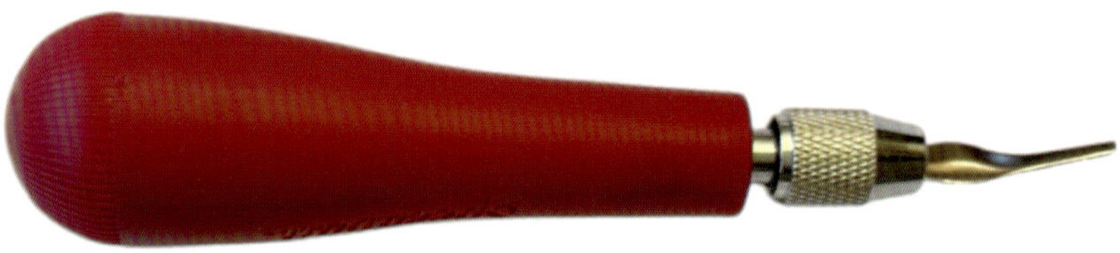

Ranger
ARCHIVAL INK
ENCRE D'ARCHIVES
• JET BLACK • NOIR DE JAIS •
ACID FREE · SANS ACIDE
PERMANENT INK · L'ENCRE INDÉLÉBILE
WATERPROOF · PREUVE DE L'EAU

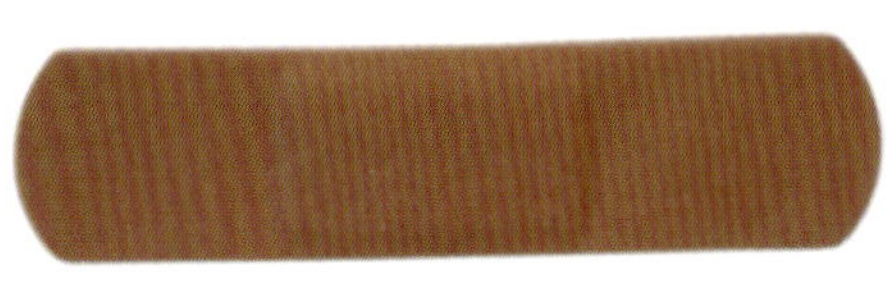

3

Getting Started: Basic Carving Safety and Knowledge

The most common response I get when I introduce people to eraser carving is a fear of the blades. "I did that in high school, and I cut myself so much!" is a repeated comment on the Internet and the reason why I only allow ages 14+ at my in-person workshops. Though I have that restriction, and have attendees sign a waiver, I don't believe that this fear should hold us or our children back from exploring and creating. I have allowed both of my children to participate in eraser carving with me while supervised in my art studio and believe that learning to work with blades is an important lesson and skill. I encourage you to breathe through any nervousness that you have about working with blades, and I will teach you some tips for successful and safe carving.

Holding the Eraser Safely

When working with such a small surface and small tools, the sharp carving blades will come very close to your fingers. This is naturally part of working small. My methods teach you how to use both hands in tandem to create intricate cuts, so it is important to learn how to hold your eraser safely. When you begin to carve, it is instinctual to hold the eraser between the thumb and forefinger, as we grasp most things in this way. When you do this, you want to be mindful of where your fingers are in relation to the blade and the direction you are carving.

Tip 1

Never hold the eraser directly where you are carving.

Tip 2

Carve away from yourself as much as possible.

Tip 3

Lay your hand flat on the table and hold the eraser between your forefinger and middle finger to secure the eraser.

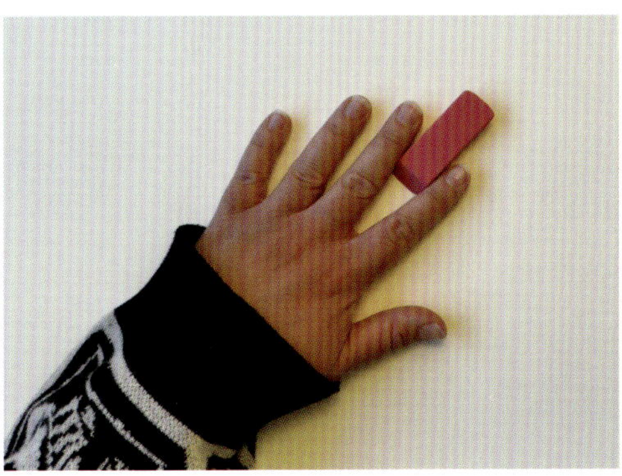

Tip 4

Don't carve too deeply into the eraser on your first pass. This requires more pressure, and more pressure gives you more chance to slip, and you will slip with more speed if you are pushing harder into the blade. Hold the blade almost entirely parallel with the eraser surface for the easiest carving, requiring less pressure.

Tracing Your Eraser for Sketches

The very first thing that I do before I begin any sketch is trace my eraser onto my paper or sketchbook several times. Erasers are a more elongated shape than artists typically design within, and instead of erasing over and over as I work on my tiny sketches, I trace the eraser three or four times so I can work through my composition in a flow. I make a couple of mock-ups before finalizing and transferring my sketch.

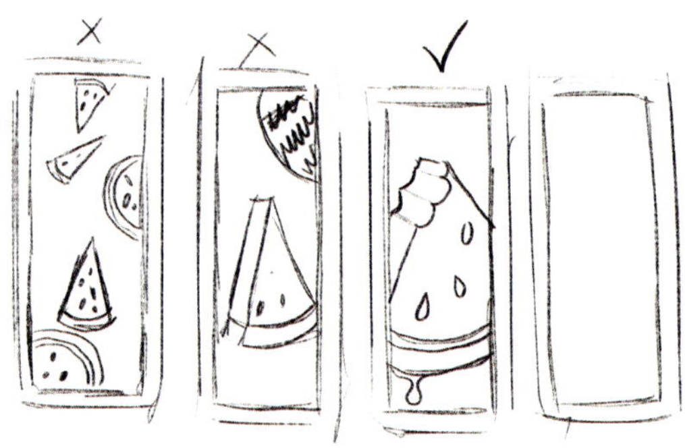

Drawing Directly onto the Eraser or Not?

There is something I find wildly freeing about this medium. I am comfortable working spontaneously and so I don't always plan out my design on paper before I begin. Allowing myself this freedom to sketch directly onto the eraser has also caused me to feel more open to creating when I am in an unusual place or have limited time. I have sketched out artwork directly onto the tiny surface of an eraser while sitting in bleachers while my daughter's track team ran circles around me, or while sitting on the edge of a basketball court while they ran drills. Some of my favorite designs came from just sitting down and creating without a plan. I have also found myself without spare paper to sketch on, and drawing straight onto the eraser surface was my only choice. I have even done this with pen, when my pencils mysteriously disappeared.

The truth about art is that all rules are made up and regularly broken, and our personal creative time should look however we want it to. If sketching your design into a notebook before you begin is what allows you to create often and with joy, then that's what you should do. But if you find yourself itching to get creative while you're sitting in the school pick-up line, you can absolutely make it up as you go and enjoy creating without a plan.

Different Blade Sizes, Shapes and Uses

Finding the right tool for a new craft can often feel intimidating, but when it comes to eraser carving, fancy, expensive tools are not needed—it is the little, inexpensive, beginner tool sets that are going to serve you best. The ideal set of blades for carving miniature prints into erasers are the ones with interchangeable blades that you will find at any art and craft store. These sets are designed to be compact, which makes them easy to store and take out and about. The small size of the handle and blades work well with the miniature surface of the eraser, and the Speedball set even stores the blades inside the handle itself, which is perfect for packing your creative go bag.

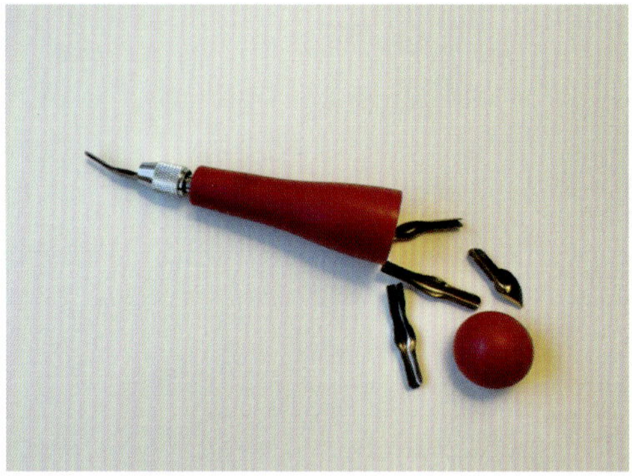

One of the best parts of carving erasers is how much softer rubber is than linoleum. It is incredibly satisfying to slice through the soft rubber with a new set of blades; because of that softness, high-end blades you might use for carving linoleum are not needed. In fact, the compact nature of these small carving blade sets allows for greater dexterity and accuracy in creating fine details on a miniature level. I find that longer carving blades, even with miniature blade sizes, cause your hand to be farther away from the eraser surface, and this affects your ability to make tiny, controlled movements while you create. In this art medium, less truly is more.

The linoleum cutter set by Speedball has the tiniest blade of all (size 1) that will quickly become the most-used blade in your tool set. If you

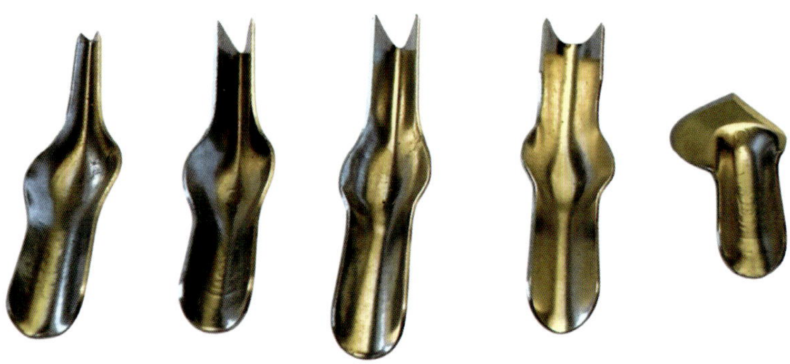

are shopping for other brands, you will want to look for the smallest V-shaped blades you can to achieve the finest details. U-shaped blades are best for removing large areas of your design but will not create fine lines. Knife-shaped blades are perfect for cutting away excess eraser to create a shaped stamp or for simply cutting your eraser into smaller pieces if needed. Before purchasing your carving blade set, ensure that small V-shaped blades are included. If you purchase a set with U-shaped blades only, you are going to be limited in your ability to create tiny art.

How to Carve Straight Lines

Carving with confidence is the best way to achieve clean cuts and sharp lines. Just as with drawing, if you overthink your line and go slowly, it is more likely to wobble. Choosing your line and carving without hesitation makes for clean cuts, but so does the way that you hold the handle of your blade. While carving erasers, you might feel tempted to hold the blade the same way you hold a pencil.

Instead, hold the handle of your carving blade the way a violinist holds a bow.

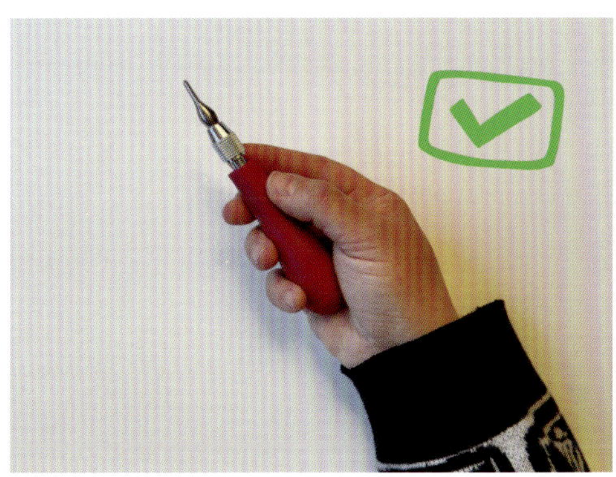

Hold the handle firmly, not too tight, and allow the line of the handle and blade to become an extension of your arm. As you carve, keep your wrist straight and align the blade to follow straightforward from your elbow and forearm.

As you explore more shapes, you can experiment with how to twist and turn the eraser and your wrist. However, as you practice straight lines, the best way to achieve them is to let your carving handle become an extension of your skeleton and to be confident.

It is natural for us to grip our tools too intensely when we are new to something, full of nerves, and focused on the artwork. If you find yourself holding your breath, pause, breathe, and unclench your fingers.

Sharpening Your Tools/Tool Maintenance

Caring for your tools is an important practice that allows you to use them for a long time, and many blades can be sharpened endlessly. The small interchangeable blades that come in the linoleum cutter sets are not made to be sharpened. Because of the inexpensive materials and manufacturing process, it is common that sharpening the blades can cause imperfections that may affect your carving quality. These blades are meant to be replaced, and the replacement blades are also highly affordable.

It is important to keep your blades sharp, as dull blades will cause your eraser surface to shred, which make them unable to achieve clean cuts. Also, having to press harder on the blade to carve the surface can cause you to slip and injure yourself. It is important to always place the blades into the handle or container they come with when not in use. Leaving a blade on the handle or allowing them to bounce around in the bottom of your go bag can cause the edges to bend, which will also shred your eraser surface and ruin your artwork. Loose blades can also be a safety hazard, so be sure to put them away properly when not in use, even if they are in a pouch or kit. If you are using blades that can be sharpened and polished, you will want to follow the manufacturer's instructions on how to maintain the sharp edge safely and correctly.

Building Your To-Go Kit

One of the great joys of creating tiny artwork is the ability to take it out into the world with you. It isn't practical to carry a large piece of linoleum to a public park or coffee shop but when your art supplies can fit into your purse or your back pocket, creating out in the world becomes much simpler and more welcoming. I call my pink eraser art kit my go bag, because I often snatch it up and toss it into my bag as I head out the door. I even keep my carving go bag on a shelf by my front door. Creativity is easier to access when we make it simple for ourselves to do so, and making the process simpler makes it more enjoyable. I have spent time carving while camping in canyons and on top of mountains, in the woods, in the desert, while waiting in the car at school pick up, while traveling, in coffee shops and treat shops, beside pools, and on patios. I can say with confidence that I have grown as an artist because of the amount of time I have spent practicing carving tiny artwork, and I have been able to devote that time practicing because I made it easy to take my art supplies with me. Also, getting out of our home and art studios is sometimes the best way to find inspiration.

Finding Inspiration

We live in an absolutely breathtaking world, surrounded by color and nature and shape and sound. I will 100 percent admit that, for me, the hardest part about being an artist is trying to choose what to draw. Why is it so hard? It is because I become overwhelmed with ideas and freeze. Sometimes I do that awful thing where I think, "Everyone draws flowers, the world doesn't need another flower drawing." Can we agree to knock that thought out of our minds? The truth is that the world can never have too many flower drawings. Flowers are amazing and only live for a brief time and deserve the honor of being observed and immortalized. Draw flowers. Also, we should never let other people's art practice affect our own ability to create. If I didn't draw flowers because of the flower art that already exists in the world, I would never learn to draw flowers. Everything we choose to draw takes us one step closer to being the artist we have always wanted to be.

When I decided to carve one hundred erasers into art prints, I released my inherent need to evaluate inspiration for its worthiness. When I chose to create art by quantity, I cared less about the meaning behind the artwork and learned to just create. I didn't go down my usual road of overthinking what I was going to draw. I didn't analyze the meaning of the object I chose to draw so intensely that I froze and wasted my precious time in my head instead of using my hands. Deciding to create a large number of artworks taught me to let go of deeper meanings and simply look out into the world and pick something. Of course, it is beautiful to create art that has deep meaning, but when we are learning, the practice itself is worthy of our time and materials. By giving myself the goal to just make something to get closer to my goal of one hundred, I released my art from judgement and allowed myself to draw anything I wanted.

Perhaps some people will read the preceding paragraph and scoff because in the heart of the artist numbers mean nothing and inspiration and meaning is everything. The truth is that I spent more time thinking about art I wanted to make and not actually making anything because I was thinking so hard I got stuck. Letting the deeper meaning of artwork go, and focusing on just making the thing, helped me to get out of my own head and work with my hands. I have gained skills and grown as an artist, and that creativity has since flowed out of me and into people all over the world all because I pushed myself to draw silly things like avocados, flowers, and cartoon characters or whatever was laying on my desk that day. Focusing on a number stopped me from overthinking, cured my anxiety about making "worthy" art, and helped me create a whole new medium for the world.

When people ask, as they often do, where I get my inspiration for my tiny eraser art carvings, the answer is: my life.

I look around my life. I choose something from the day, or something nearby, or the food I ate for lunch. Sometimes it is something from my childhood, or a cartoon my children were watching (oh, I'm just kidding,

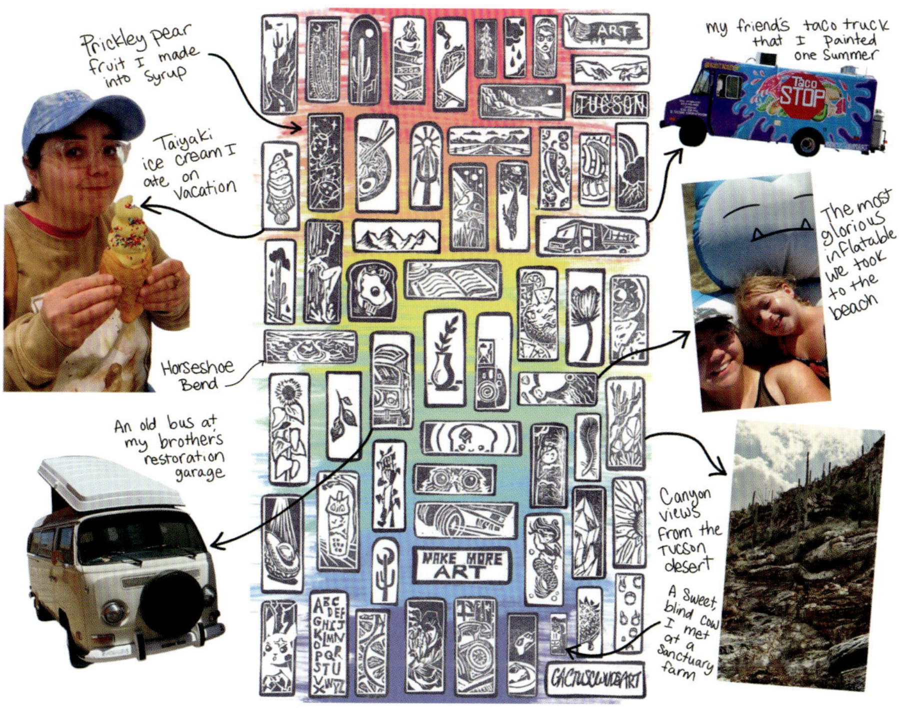

the Pokémon I carve are all from the cartoon I was watching, let's be real). My favorite eraser design carvings are a Taiyaki ice cream I ate at a shop, my Nintendo switch, fried eggs, and a vintage VW bus my brother had at his restoration garage one day. I have also carved based on something I wanted to try, such as curves, so I carved a word in cursive. I once carved a jar of fireflies, because I was goofing off and stabbing my eraser and loved the shapes my ballpoint pen left behind. I carved a jar around them (but I left the lid open so they could breathe).

Finding inspiration can start simply, like finding a list of prompts from an online challenge. It can grow into having the confidence to draw the latte you are sipping in a coffee shop. Suddenly, you will find yourself witnessing something that stops you in your tracks, like a full moon shining on pine trees at the top of a mountain and realize that you are already picturing how you will recreate the vision on that little block of rubber. Allowing yourself to carve random things will give you the practice and experience you need to create anything. So don't think too hard about it, pick something, and draw.

Tip

Pack it out! Every scrap. Taking our carving set go bags out into the world is exhilarating, but it is important to collect every scrap of rubber, place it into your go bag, and pack it out. Taking art into the world is great for us, but we need to make sure it is also great for our environment and wildlife.

4

Border or No Border?

This is the first question I answer in every single workshop and demonstration, and it is an important one. I draw a border around every eraser that I carve for several reasons—I will tell you why, and then that the choice is ultimately up to you. Let's go!

Creating a Collection

The first reason that I established the border around my eraser art is because I wanted something stylistic to connect all of my artwork. I have ADHD. Because of my ADHD, my artwork and style and interests change drastically and quickly and can make it hard for people to identify my artwork. When I began carving erasers, I wanted to incorporate something that would be recognizable to viewers across the Internet, regardless of subject matter or style. As my collection of miniature artworks has grown over time, the consistency of the border has made them a cool collection of work. It ties them together when framed and hung as miniature gallery walls in people's homes, it makes them look very cool when stamped together in a collage-style artwork, and it has served its purpose in tying my vastly varying subjects together aesthetically.

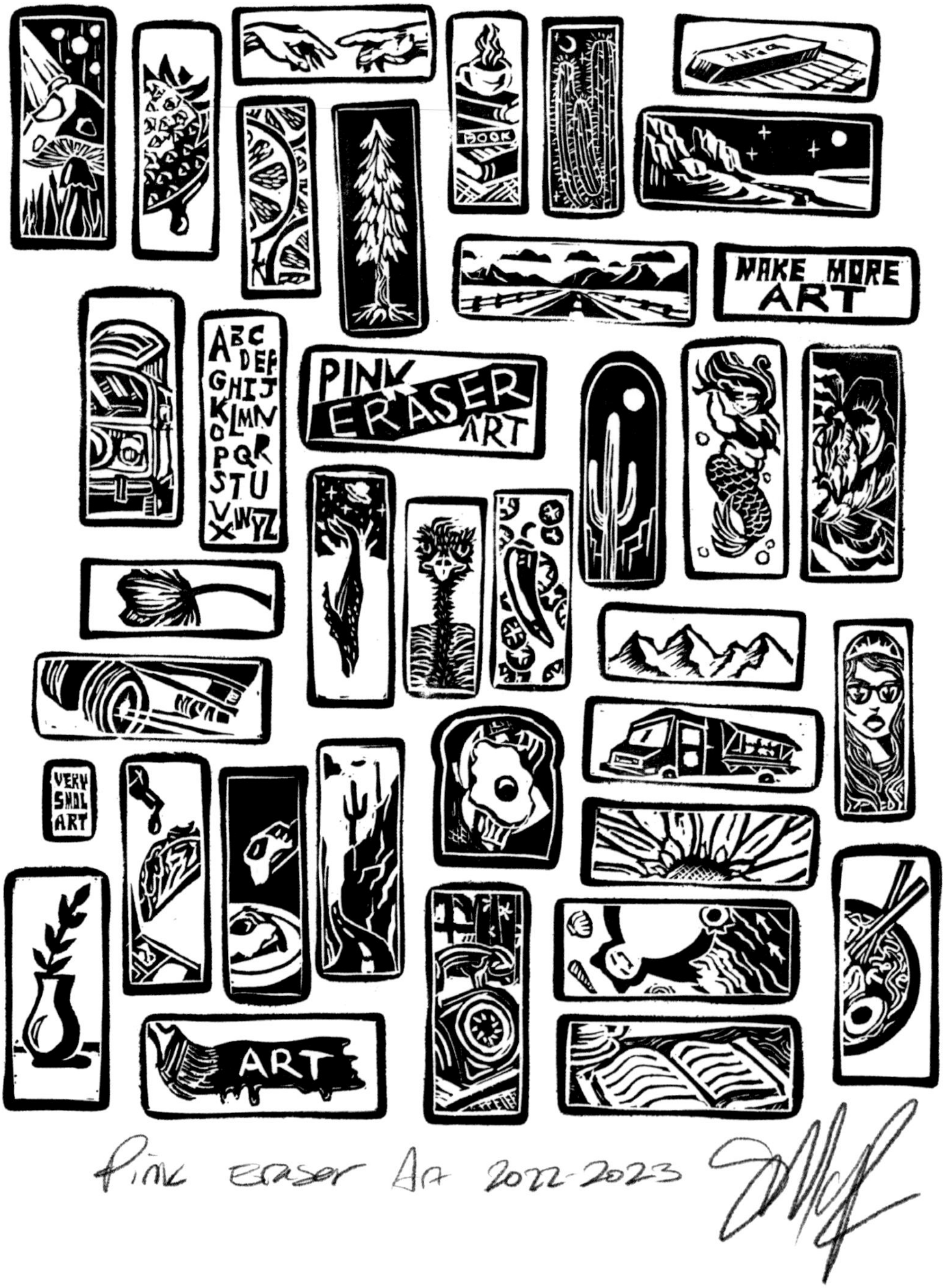
MAKE MORE ART
PINK ERASER ART
ABCDEFGHIJKLMNOPQRSTUVWXYZ
BOOK
VERY SMOL ART
ART
Pink Eraser Art 2022-2023

Beating Blank-Page Anxiety

Beginning the artwork with a border is a creative tool that helps me be fearless in the process. Getting started with a new print can feel intimidating as you face a new, fresh surface, as you decide which areas to carve away and which areas to leave behind, and as you face making the first cut. We already talked about blank-page anxiety, which is the fear of making the first mark on a blank surface. I find that by beginning every piece with the same motions I allay any fears or anxieties that hold me back from creating. I don't need to overthink how to start a piece when I start every piece with four straight lines.

A Finished Look

I particularly love the border because then every eraser stamp I make is already a perfectly framed piece of artwork. It gives a finished look to the art, and honors it with a frame, no matter where it is stamped. My eraser carving prints have been framed beautifully with beveled matte boards cut to tiny sizes, but they have also adorned pages in my planners, journals, and sketchbooks. The tiny frame makes my miniature artworks stand boldly no matter where or how they are displayed.

Support for Clean Printing

There is actually a technical reason why I love utilizing a border around my eraser art carvings—it helps create a clean print. Eraser rubber is very soft, and when printing or stamping your tiny artwork, it is easy to add too much pressure, causing ink smudges around the design or in the negative spaces that you want to stay clear. The border works as a support; it stops the stamp from rocking to either side, and holds the stamp even during printing, allowing for the cleanest print possible.

Borders: It's Up to You

Whether or not to create a border around your artwork is entirely up to you. If you choose not to create a border, and still want to ensure the cleanest print possible, you can cut away excess eraser that could transfer ink where you don't want it to be. You can also explore ways of manipulating the border artistically, such as bringing your artwork to the foreground by cutting out areas of the border or changing the shape of the border by where you carve it on the eraser surface. For now, let's get into the basics of relief carving and explore breaking out of the border later on.

Borders to Try

I create my borders in one way, but it isn't the only way. When carving with my child, we make wavy borders. You can make your borders textured, messy, or checkered. It is up to you. Here are a few ideas to get you started:

Standard Border

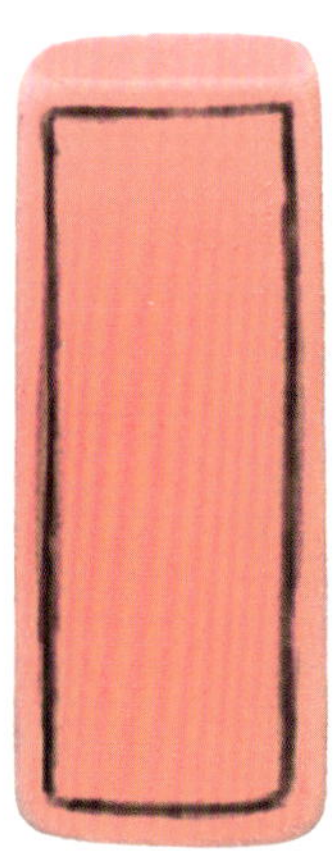

Crossed Lines Border

Wavy Border

Blanket Stitch Border

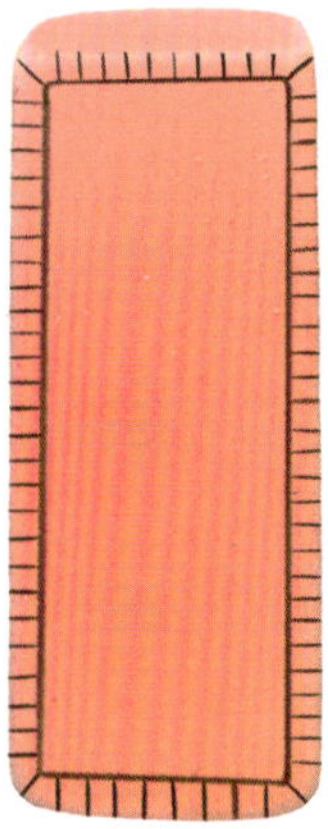

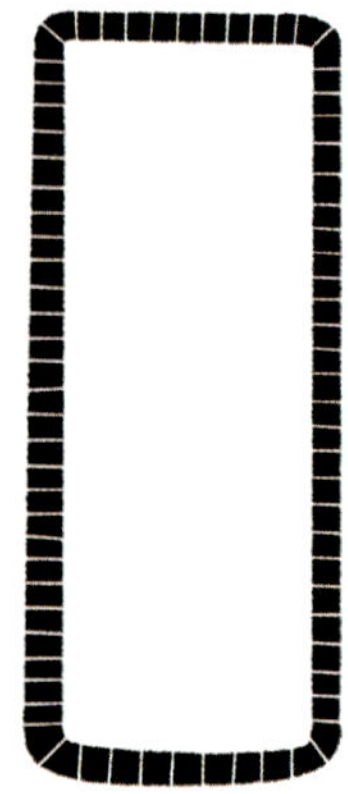

Checkered Border

5

Positive and Negative Space

This is the hardest part of printmaking, and I am going to help you. I was recently sitting next to my college roommate at an art conference, watching a demonstration on relief design. Tears slowly gathered in her eyes as she tried to wrap her head around utilizing positive and negative space in relief art, and it was an absolute delight to witness. I still remember my one and only art class in college, and the way learning to think in positive and negative space was breaking my own brain until we did one activity that made it suddenly make sense. The feeling of the lightbulb moment when learning a new art skill is one of my favorite things in life, and hands-on practice is essential to reach that moment. Please do not allow yourself to give up before you begin if this doesn't make immediate sense to you!

Here it is in a nutshell: we are working with a printing style called "relief art." We are carving away parts of a flat surface and using what is left behind to print a design. Understanding positive and negative space is an essential skill to be able to explore the lessons in this book and to begin creating your own eraser art prints. But don't worry, because even if you don't get it right now, understanding will come to you as you begin to practice carving and stamping. My college roommate was still baffled as we left the art conference demonstration, but the next day we signed up for a hands-on lesson, and she was then able to create a beautiful piece of relief art. Even if this section feels confusing, stick through the lessons in this book and I promise you will be able to make stellar art by the end!

Understanding Positive and Negative Space

Positive and negative space is an empowering tool once you understand how to manipulate it in your designs. The ways you use it can literally turn an artwork from night to day. For the majority of the projects in this book we will be working with black ink and white paper, so I will regularly refer to "black" and "white" even though your own ink and paper could be any color.

Positive space: any untouched area on your carving surface that will transfer ink during printing. This is what is left behind after you finish carving. Throughout the lessons in this book, positive space will be anything that is black on the page, as these areas will transfer the black ink I love to use.

Negative space: the areas that are removed during the carving process. Negative space can be large areas or tiny details; any space cut away from the eraser surface is considered negative space and will not transfer ink during printing. On your prints, negative space will ultimately be whatever the color of your surface is. I will exclusively be using white paper, so throughout the lessons in this book, the negative space will be the white areas.

As I sketch out my designs, I consider how I want to utilize positive and negative space. Do I want to carve everything out and just create a line-drawing-style stamp? Do I want it to be bold, dark, and striking and only carve out the lines of my sketch? Do I want the landscape to be seen as night, and leave the sky as positive space, which will print in black, or do I want to carve the sky away so the negative space will be daytime in the artwork?

As you plan your sketch, it can be helpful to color in the positive space areas.

Night or Day?

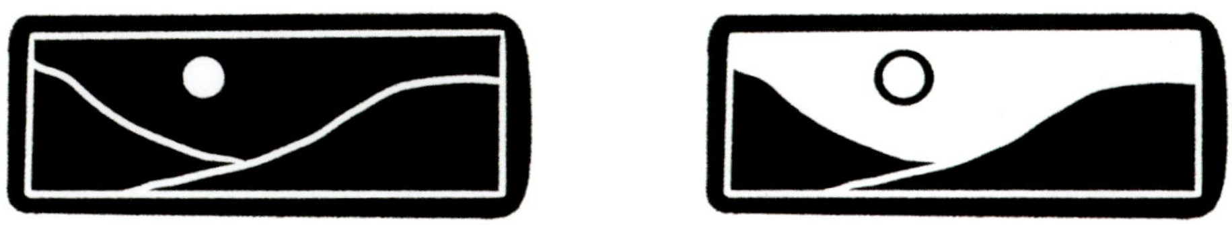

I am a firm believer in putting ideas into practice to really understand them, so let's carve the same design in two different ways: one will be night and one will be day. We will accomplish this by using positive and negative space.

The Drawing

1. Draw your border if you plan to use one.

2. Draw a circle in the top half of the eraser. This will be either our sun or our moon.

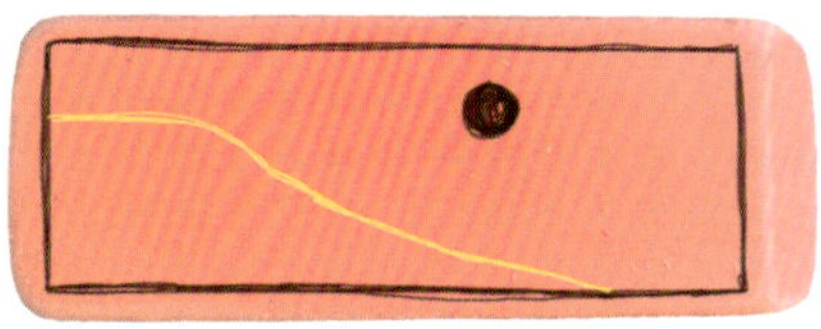

3. Draw a line from the upper left of your eraser down to the bottom right of your eraser to create a mountain in the foreground.

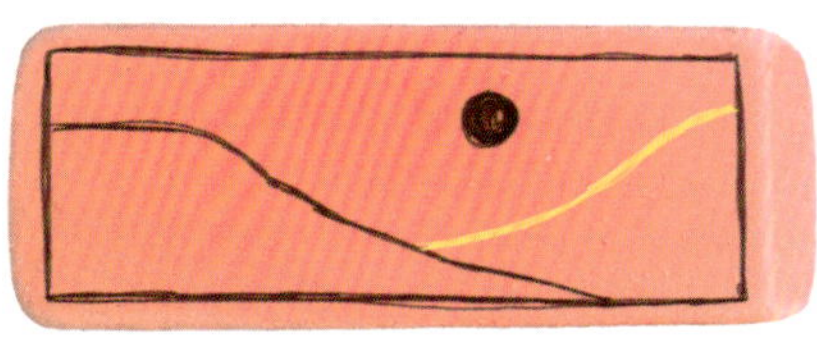

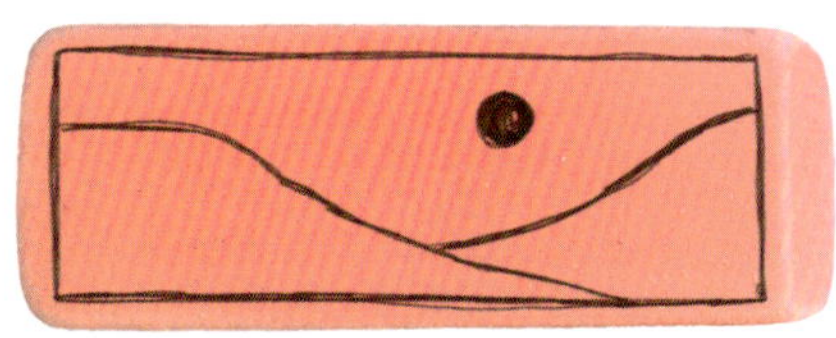

4. Draw a line from the upper right of your eraser down to the center, touching the first line, to create a mountain in the background.

The Carving

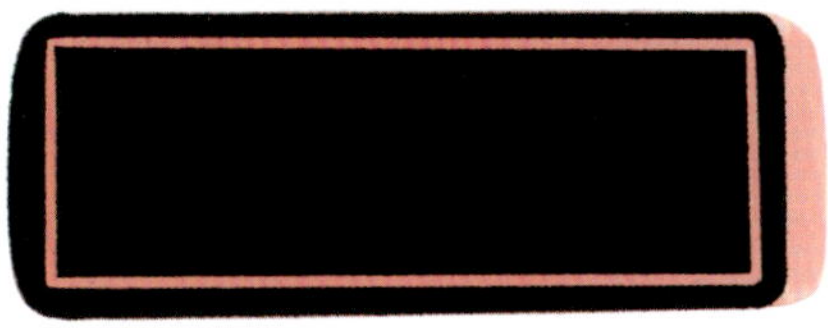

5. Carve your border if you are using one.

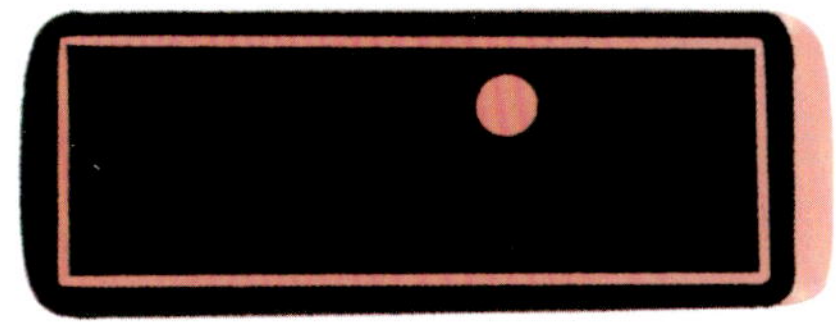

6. Carve out the small circle that is your sun/moon by pressing the tip of your carver into the eraser and spinning it in a circle. There are tips on this in chapter 10, but this is the first lesson, so feel free to just dive in to figure out this concept.

7. Carve over the two mountain lines.
8. At this point you have your mountain landscape in the dark of night. The positive space of the sky will transfer ink to your paper, making it a nighttime scene.

9. Carve a circle around your moon.

10. Carve out the entirety of the sky.
11. Now you have turned your nighttime scene into a daytime scene. The sky is now made of negative space, which will not transfer ink during printing.

Tips for Using Positive and Negative Space

Color in the positive-space areas while planning your sketch, and when you transfer your sketch to the eraser surface. It can be easy to accidentally carve where you shouldn't, and if you do, there is no going back.

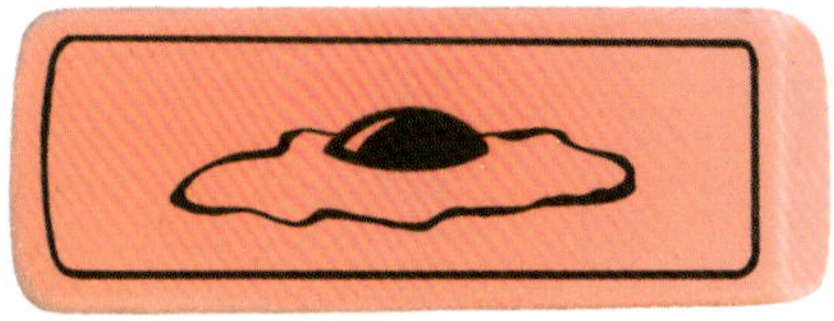

Use negative space to create daylight, sunny skies, or highlights. Use positive space for night skies and shadow.

When deciding what parts of your design should be positive or negative space, begin with any details of your design that are inherently light or dark. For example, if your artwork has an egg, egg-whites should be white!

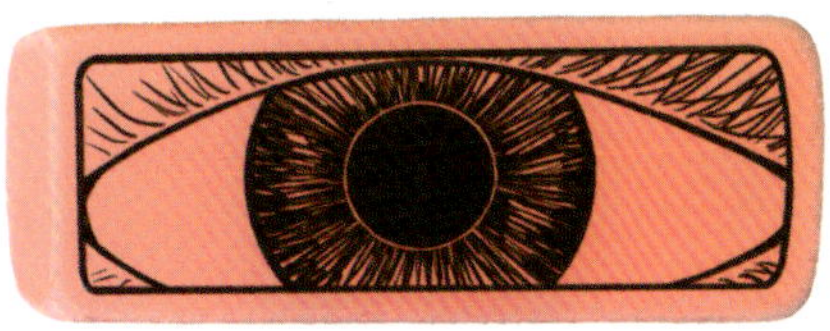

That is an easy detail to choose to carve out first. On the flip side, if you are creating an eye, you know you want the pupil to be black, so you can immediately color that in and work out the design from there.

To help you see a clear contrast between positive and negative space as you carve, you can color your eraser surface with a marker before you begin carving and after you finalize your sketch. Using a contrasting color will help you to see your cuts more clearly as you work. Do not use a permanent marker so that you can wipe it away if needed.

Finalize your sketch.

Color your eraser surface with a contrasting color.

Wipe away excess ink to leave a tint.

Carve.

6

Transferring Your Design onto an Eraser

When making your art process your own you can do whatever you want, but if you have a sketch that you want to get just right, you can transfer it to your eraser surface instead of having to draw it all over again. There are a couple of different ways to do this: with pencil and paper or from a digital drawing.

IMPORTANT NOTE

Everything that you design and carve onto your eraser will print with a mirror image. This means that if you have text, or any details that need to face a specific direction, it is important to make note that it is mirrored on your eraser surface before you begin carving. To clarify, if you have text in your design, it needs to be backward when you carve it into the eraser in order to be forward when printed. For both of the following transfer methods, if your design is the correct direction, it will be mirrored when transferred onto the eraser. It is only when drawing directly onto the eraser that you need to mirror the image while drawing.

Method One: Transferring Pencil Sketch from Paper to Eraser

Number 2 graphite pencils are your best friend for transferring sketches from your paper to the eraser. Here are the steps:

1. Trace your eraser onto the page.

2. Finalize your sketch.

3. Line the eraser up on top of the sketch.

4. Fold the paper up tightly against the edge of your eraser.

5. Fold the paper again, against the top of the eraser.

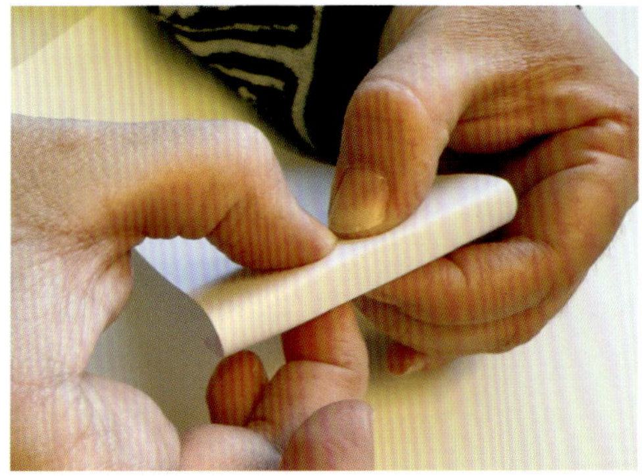

6. Holding the paper firmly against the eraser, you can now flip the paper and eraser over without it shifting.

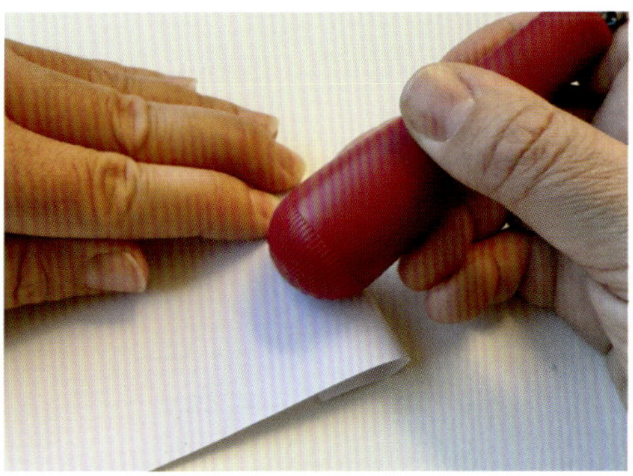

7. Use the rounded handle of your carver to rub the back of the pencil sketch to transfer the graphite sketch onto the eraser surface.

8. Uncover your eraser.

Method Two: Toner Transfers for Digital Art

Any digital art piece can be transferred to the eraser surface when printed with a toner printer with the use of acetone and a cotton swab. This method is ideal when creating multiple erasers with the same sketch for use in classrooms or groups carving together.

1. Using your digital illustration software, design your artwork in the correct size to fit the eraser when printed from your toner printer. This step is entirely up to you, based on your programs and printer models.
2. Print your image from your toner printer.
3. Line your eraser up on top of the image.

4. Fold the paper up tightly against the edge of your eraser.

5. Fold the paper again, against the top of the eraser.

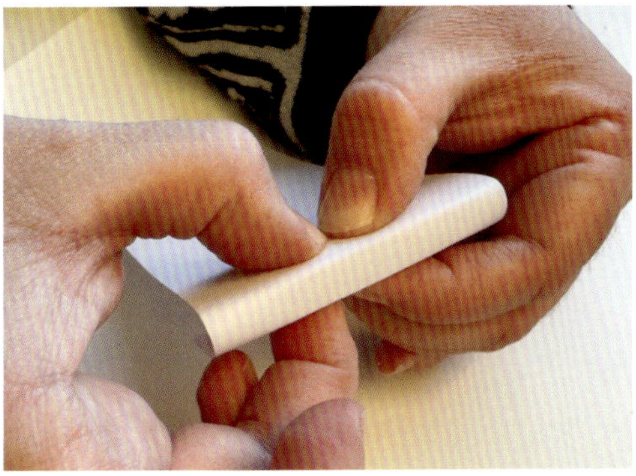

6. Holding the paper firmly against the eraser, you can now flip the paper and eraser over without it shifting.

7. While holding the paper tightly in place and flush against the eraser surface, dab the back of the paper with a cotton swap soaked in acetone (i.e., nail polish remover). Ensure the paper does not shift.

8. When the paper is thoroughly soaked through with acetone, lift the paper gently to check if the image has successfully transferred, if not, lower it back down and apply gentle pressure to the paper with your cotton swab.

9. Remove the paper, lifting it away from the surface, so you do not smudge the toner transfer. Once it is dry, which should happen quickly, you can begin to carve your eraser.

Tip

If you do not have access to a toner printer, you can print your image out in the correct size, cover all of the black areas with graphite from a number 2 pencil, and then follow through with a rubbing transfer.

7

Carving Depth

One common question I am asked about carving so small is how I manage to get the level of detail on such a tiny surface. The answer is using the right blades and how deeply I carve into the surface. The eraser's softness makes carving at different depths fun and easy.

When carving a design, I have three different depths that I carve to. This is not highly technical, and has its pros and cons, but here it is:

Depth 1: Tiniest details

Depth 2: The first pass

Depth 3: Cleaning it up

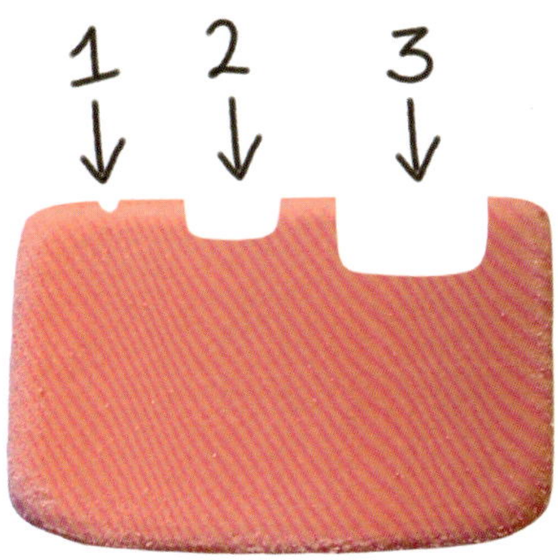

As you begin to carve into erasers, I urge you to breathe and enjoy the feel of it. It is incredibly satisfying and soothing to do, and though I am showing you a diagram and teaching you about my fine-tuned artistic and technical choices, everything comes down to simply choosing to have fun and enjoy yourself. Now that I have coached you into not overthinking it, let's overthink it together.

Step One: The First Pass

As you make your first passes over your design, remember to hold your blade parallel with the eraser surface. Depending on the level of detail, and how much eraser you are removing, you may be using a V- or U-shaped blade. I almost always begin every carving with a size 2 V-shaped blade from Speedball. As I create my initial cuts into the eraser, especially if using a V-shaped blade, there will be raised carving lines after I have removed the first layer of the relief design. If I leave these raised edges from the carving lines, they will inevitably transfer ink onto my print when the design is stamped. Some artists use these carving lines as part of their design, but we will get into that stylistic choice later. If we want the cleanest print possible, we need to remove a deeper layer of our eraser.

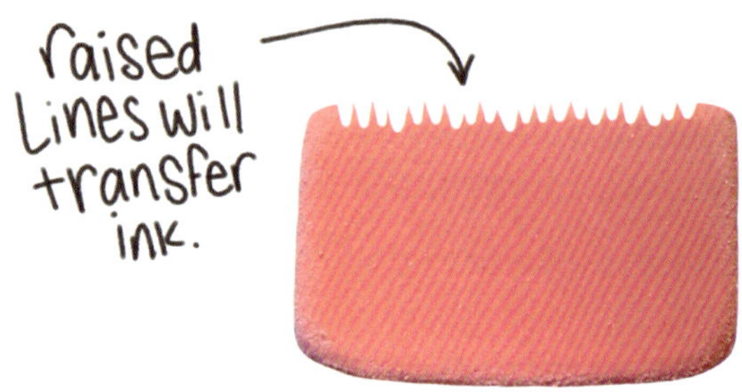

Step Two: Cleaning It Up

After my first pass, I switch from the V-shaped blade to the U-shaped blade and use its rounded nature to carve deeper into my eraser, smoothing out the initial carving lines. If this is done mindfully, you should achieve a clean print, even with hand-printing using a good level of pressure.

Step Three: The Finest Details

Finally, after removing the largest areas, cutting deeper and smoothing out the carve lines, I use the smallest V-shaped blade (size 1) by Speedball and carve out the finest details. The trick to my finest details, is that I use this blade to literally scrape the surface more than carve. I have tested simply scraping the surface as lightly as possible with the smallest blade and still managed to make a legible piece of artwork.

There is one con to working with such fine details and that is the inability to print with different inks. I have found that the finest details are so shallow that they cannot be printed with standard printing ink and a brayer. The ink is slightly thicker and so fills in the fine lines and obscures them. When printing with an ink pad, however, the finest details can be printed clean and clear.

NOTE

When carving with a V-shaped blade, you can achieve different widths with a single blade based entirely on the pressure of your cuts. Lighter pressure makes thinner lines while more pressure will cut deeper, making thicker lines.

8

Composition: Framing Your Image

Carving stamps can be as simple as drawing a picture and carving it out, but what turns a simple object or design from a stamp into a tiny work of art is composition. Before I begin, I have to say that carving out an object to make a stamp is worthy and good, and awesome, and not at all lesser than what I am about to teach you. That said, creating a stamp with composition in mind can turn this silly little art medium from an embellishment into compelling, fine art. We can use this minimally sized surface to create artwork that draws the eye just as effectively as a large painting on canvas does.

The Rule of Thirds

The rule of thirds is such a forefront rule in the world of art and design that it may be something you have heard, even if you don't consider yourself an artist. It is such a common rule it is even programmed into your phone's camera. Have you ever wondered what the lines across the image are when taking a photograph with your phone? They are guidelines to help you line up your image using the rule of thirds!

Let's look at this example from my own phone camera.

You'll see that the horizontal and vertical lines are splitting the image into thirds, from top to bottom and left to right. We could get deep into mathematics and art history, but instead we are going to keep it simple. See where the lines meet and cross each other? Those are the areas that turn art into magic.

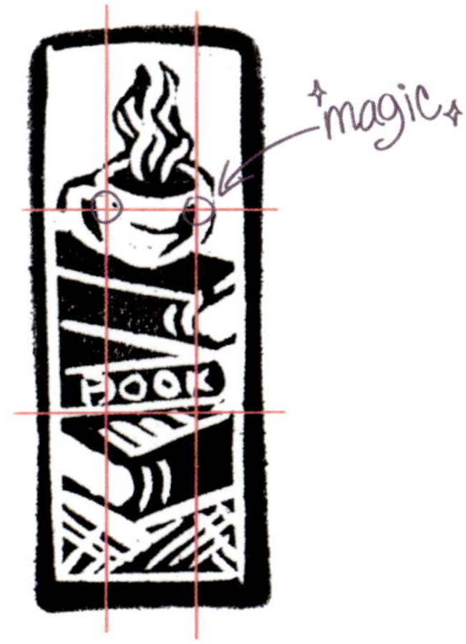

What does that mean, and how do you use it? When creating your composition, instead of placing your subject right in the middle, place the focal point, the subject, or the main detail where the lines cross. You can put your areas of interest on a single cross-point, or spread across two, which is mostly how we work on the tiny surfaces of our erasers. In the figure below, the subject is placed in the center of the eraser.

In the next figure, the subject is placed using the rule of thirds. You'll see that there is more negative space to one side, which already invites our eyes to wander across the image instead of standing still in the center of the art.

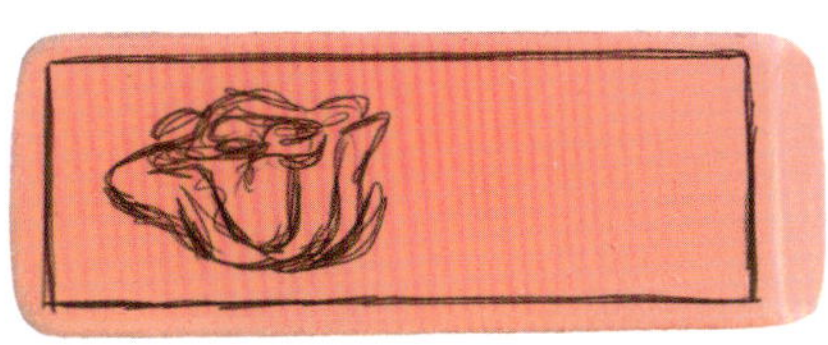

In figure three, I added background details that also land in the rule of thirds markings, adding motion to the composition and drawing the eye back to the subject.

Front and Center

Now that we have covered the rule of thirds, I get to tell you to break it. It may be called the rule of thirds, but remember that in artistic exploration, rules are just guidelines. The joy of creating is exploring ideas, making something, and seeing how we like it. It is fine, great, even, to try one design in multiple ways. That is where sketching your idea first will serve you, so you can try multiple compositions.

While the rule of thirds invites the eye to wander and linger on a piece of artwork, putting your subject front and center can be striking and powerful in an impactful way. Let me tell you about the chicken that went viral. I drew this silly, little chicken and I placed it exactly centered in the frame, with a big head and a little body, because I wanted to create the feeling that he was just staring up at you in the most adorable way.

This little chicken had viewers online commenting that he was staring from the void into their souls. He had shaken them with his intensity. The portrait of this silly little guy made more of an impact on viewers because he was centered, creating the effect of him being up in your face. Had I placed his little face in the crosses of the rule of thirds grid, his stare would have been less intense because there would not be the effect of him imposing on your space. By removing excess blank area around the subject, he effectively invaded your personal bubble.

In the next section, we will look at centering your subject without invading anyone's personal space and just honoring the shape and detail of the subject. You can create detail around the subject in this style, but by choosing to carve out the background as cleanly as possible, framing your object of focus perfectly centered in the frame creates a graphic, pop-art vibe that is bold and striking.

Breaking the Frame

(Insert "thinking outside the box" pun here.) If you choose to create a frame around your tiny art pieces, that doesn't mean it has to be a barrier keeping the artwork enclosed. A frame doesn't have to become a cage for your creative expression, or, more literally, for your art. As you plan your design, try allowing some detail of it to break through the frame. Let a leaf or a flower petal continue past the border. This creates a feeling of depth as the subject matter reaches beyond the frame, creating a new, unexpected foreground. This is especially effective when you allow parts of your design to be contained by the border while setting other parts of your design free. This is also a design element that can be used to bring multiple designs together as a collection, as you can see in my series of flower carvings.

Reshaping the Frame

While standard pink erasers are rectangles it is very freeing to realize that we don't have to make all eraser art into rectangles. I love recognizing the original shape of the eraser in my carvings, which is part of why I create a frame around every piece of eraser art that I carve. It is my nod to the medium itself. But your frames and borders do not need to follow the same rules. One of my most popular eraser carvings is loved because I re-created the expected edges of the rectangle eraser into an archway.

I curved two of the corners. On another piece, I brought one side of the border closer to the center in order to allow space for the tail of a speech bubble. As you plan your design, you can manipulate the border to create new shapes while still utilizing the natural border of the eraser, or you can break out of the rectangle and create your own new shapes entirely.

Using Guidelines to Compose Your Design

When I start laying out my design on my sketch paper, or directly onto my eraser, I always draw a few guidelines before I begin. Guidelines create an outline that you can use to make sure your sketch stays within the borders of the eraser surface. It helps you know where to draw the focal point and work within the unusual boundaries that come with creating on a small, usually elongated surface.

Marking Your Focal Point

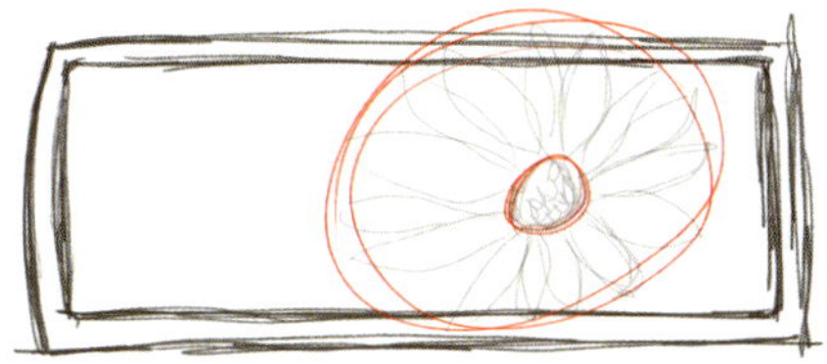

My guidelines may look different depending on the design, but, in general, I draw a circle where I want my focal point. If I am drawing a flower, I make a circle where the center of the flower will land and a larger circle around that where the petals will end.

If I'm drawing a bird, I make a little circle where the head will go and a larger circle where the body will be.

Doing this ensures that, as I create my sketch, I won't accidentally draw the face of the bird off the edge of the eraser. Taking a moment to give yourself a loose boundary before you start your actual sketch can save a lot of grief.

Triangles and Threes

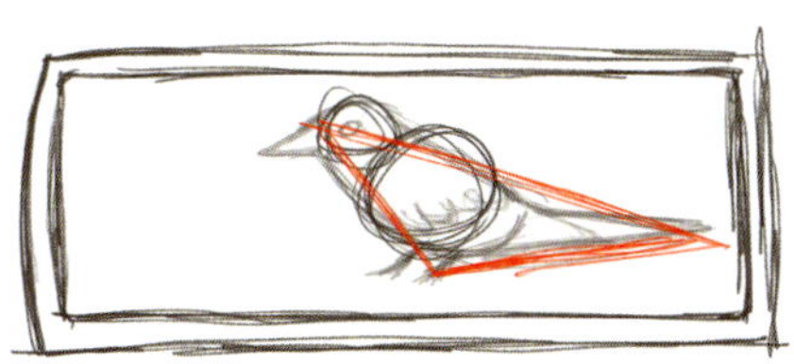

Triangles are the strongest way to build a bridge and also the strongest way to create a simple composition. Remember how we just discussed the rule of thirds being a magic recipe for intriguing compositions? That was a rule for how to split up the plane of our canvas (or eraser), but there is an additional tip that lives within the magic number three when creating an arrangement of subjects.

Art loves triangles. After I decide on a focal point, I almost always use a triangle to compose the rest of the image, anchoring one tip of the triangle within the focal point marker. We decided where the head and body of the bird will go, and now we can use the triangle to decide the angle of the tail, feet, and beak.

If we are creating an arrangement of flowers and leaves, we can draw a triangle and place the subjects on each tip, or arrange them within the triangle, like this example with the bunch of lemons.

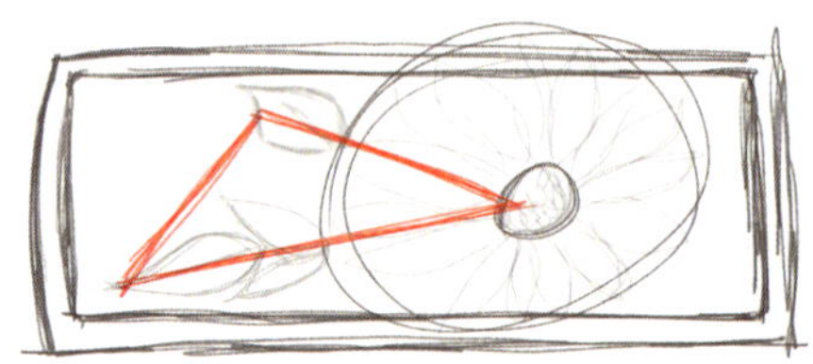

If you find yourself struggling to make a sketch feel balanced, try working the design into a triangle guideline and see if you find the harmony you are looking for.

Enhancing Composition with Extra Detail

The rule of thirds is magic, but sometimes we definitely don't feel like negative space is the vibe. In these situations, if we feel brave enough to create tiny artworks within our tiny artwork, we can add a background or additional detail that draws the eye to and compliments our subject. This can be as simple as adding a couple of sparkle shapes; cartoon-style movement lines; or a cute, little heart. It

can also be adding a waft of smoke around a flame, or water splashing away from the subject. It could be a vine of leaves or just some texture markings. The key to using extra details to create a compelling composition that draws the eye around the image and back to the subject is in the shapes and arrangements we choose.

Activity: Practice Composition

Trace your eraser onto a sheet of paper multiple times, and then choose a single subject, like an apple, a seashell, or an acorn. You can do all of these sketches during one sit-down or try one each day as you practice your sketching and carving.

1. Rule of Thirds

   Draw your subject in the center of your first sketch. Now, draw two horizontal and two vertical lines across your second eraser sketch like the example to mark out your rule of thirds guidelines. Draw your subject in one of the crosses across the image. Notice the difference between your two sketches and see how it inspires you.

2. Front and Center

   Draw your subject as large as you can across your eraser, allowing the edges of your subject to go over the border lines. Set your subject right in the center of your eraser and notice how zooming in on your subject in this way makes it feel more imposing.

3. Breaking the Frame

   Draw your subject, allowing part of it to cross over the border line. When carving, you will carve around this part of your subject before you carve out your border. Then carve out your border, avoiding the area of your subject that is crossing it.

4. Reshaping the Frame

   Play with ways you can reshape the frame around your subject by shortening it, allowing your subject to cross outside of it, or turning your eraser shape into an oval or an archway.

5. Marking Your Focal Point

   Before drawing your subject, draw a circle where you want it to be on the sketch. If you want every detail of your subject to be within the border, make sure your guideline is inside the border. Now, use that guideline to draw your image precisely, keeping it inside the guideline, so no part of the subject extends beyond the border.

6. Triangles and Threes

   Create a circle where you want your subject to be. Now, use that circle as an anchor point for a triangle that reaches across the elongated eraser shape. Add details to your subject, placing each additional detail within the triangle angles.

   Draw a triangle across your elongated eraser shape, then draw your subjects on each of the angles, allowing the triangle to arrange your composition for you.

7. Enhancing Composition with Extra Detail

   Copy your sketch from the Rule of Thirds exercise. Now add more detail to the empty space, making the detail smaller or more ambiguous than your main subject. This can be as simple as adding some lines to create streaks in the space, or a more detailed background image. Adding water as a splash could bring movement to your subject, or a little heart could add some whimsy and personality to your subject.

9

Image Styles

This section of the book focuses on planning out your design. True story: I often draw the picture that I want and then sit back and realize I am not exactly sure how I want to actually execute it as I begin carving. The majority of my artistic expression happens on the fly, without any pre-planning, but after exploring eraser carving for a while I have established a few image styles that I have found helpful for teaching others to begin expressing themselves with the craft. You can use these image style examples to help figure out how you want to tell your story as you begin each of your eraser carving designs.

Floating Object

I was really on top of my game when I named this style while ad-libbing a tutorial on social media one day. A floating object is when you place your subject in the center of the eraser, not allowing it to touch any of the border edges, so it is floating in space. This style celebrates the form of a subject and creates a bold, graphic pop. When carving a floating object, you can add objects in the negative space around the subject, like the mermaid with her bubbles, but, overall, the nature of this style is to have the subject completely surrounded by negative space.

Line Drawing

Line drawing in carving erasers can be done in two ways and is either the easiest form of carving or the most demanding, depending on your choice of the positive and negative spaces.

The easiest way to carve any eraser design is to carve over your drawn lines. While this is the simplest way to plan out what to carve away, it does require some finesse, as every blade stroke will be visible, and it can be difficult or impossible to hide any slip-ups or mistakes.

The most demanding option is when you want a simple line drawing as a positive, which is accomplished by carving out everything around the lines of your drawing. An important tip for accomplishing this is to go over your drawing several times with your pencil to make the lines thicker. Thicker lines will be easier to carve around and will hold up to the carving process better than pencil-tip-thin lines.

Environmental

This style is defined by the creation of a full world inside the tiny border of the eraser. We don't just draw a vintage telephone; we give it a table to sit on and a floral curtain hanging around the scene we can also see out the window.

The environmental style is all about setting the scene and creating a complex story within a tiny space. Creating an environment for your subject can be as simple as a single line and a shadow to create a tabletop and a light source.

It can be the addition of wood grain on the background, to create a desktop for a book to rest on.

Creating an environment can be complex in detail or minimalist in style, but the goal is to make the viewer believe that there is a larger world behind the frame. It is the ability to turn the eraser into a window that offers a peek into another world.

Pattern

Patterns have always happened for me one of two ways: I either didn't know what else to draw so I just drew more of the first thing, or I enjoyed the detail of something so much that I wanted to do it again and again. Patterns are a great way to fill a space when you just want to carve and ideas are few. They can also be great way to practice a blade technique through repetition. And while you can carve popular patterns, such as a checkerboard, to make a stamp as a statement or fun embellishment, for me, it is simply a design with any repetitive element used to fill a space. For some reason, this has almost exclusively been used to illustrate food, but you can try it with any subject matter or even just ambiguous shapes and lines.

Tip

When carving the same thing stacked around itself in a repeating pattern, remember to carve a line around each object to define one from the other. Boundary lines give definition to your subject.

Portrait

When in doubt, carve a headshot of an emu. Portraits are a timeless classic in the practice of creating art and the rectangle shape of pink erasers lends itself to the vibe of portrait mode. You can still explore interesting framing in your portrait-style designs, so don't allow the rigidity of formal head-shots to get into your creative headspace too deeply.

Fine Line

This image style is something I began to explore after I had carved over one hundred erasers, and I found myself wondering if I could carve fine enough lines that I could actually create different values in my artwork. It is a new exploration for me that I find delightful and offer the challenge to you. This technique uses hatching and cross hatching with the shallowest cuts you can manage to create shapes, highlights, and various values, similar to sketching with a pen.

Borderless

This eraser design is set free of constraints and is easily the most classic stamp design style. Instead of capturing a whole world, or creating a framed image, a borderless design simply is what it is. Borderless stamps can be made from your classic pink eraser shape, an eraser cut into pieces, or erasers already made into fun shapes!

The borderless erasers I carved in this way were done because I found silly little eraser sets that were loaves of bread and even came delivered as such. The erasers were so cute and brought me joy, and so I just decorated them with delicious toast toppings.

It Is What It Is

Using shaped erasers is a very fun way to find inspiration. You can even carve erasers printed with illustrations to create stamps of popular characters or sayings, using the illustration printed on the eraser as your carving pattern. It is important to keep copyright laws in mind before choosing to profit off of this type of stamp carving, but for personal use it can be so much fun!

Combining Image Styles

Categorizing these image styles has been a fun way for me to teach others about composing their own designs when planning their next eraser carving, but they in no way are the limit. I always find that as soon as I begin practicing a new art medium or playing around with a certain theme or thought, my creativity begins to spark new ideas. When I allow myself the time to regularly explore an art medium it can be like kindling to a flame. As you begin to create your own compositions, consider ways you can combine these styles to create intriguing compositions that tell your story. Maybe you'll even discover your own signature style!

ART
TUCSON
MAKE MORE ART
CACTUSCLOUDART

10

Cutting Clean Lines

As you begin to carve you will be focused on figuring out your design and learning to understand how to use positive and negative space to create the image you see in your mind. Usually, it is after we carve our erasers and stamp them that we see every flaw. Then we dive into the eraser with our blade and a determination to clean up the scraggly bits, which then shreds our edges even further and sometimes destroys our artwork completely. I am going to teach you how to avoid this by ensuring you are creating clean cuts from the start.

Keep Your Blade Sharp

The most important detail; and easiest way to ensure you create clean, smooth cuts while carving; is in your preparation: make sure your blades are sharp. A dull blade will shred your eraser rubber. If you are using a carving set with interchangeable blades, these are usually designed to be replaced, not sharpened. If you are diving into a larger eraser carving project, you might consider purchasing a replacement set of blades in advance to ensure you have replacements on hand when the time comes. I carved over one hundred erasers before I replaced my blades so this isn't something you should worry about at the start. If you are using higher quality blades, you will want to check with the manufacturer regarding the best way to sharpen your blades and do it often.

Care for Your Blades

After ensuring that you are working with sharpened blades, the quality of the blades should be noted. If your blade has become bent or chipped in any way it is going to affect the quality of your cuts. I used a bent blade for a while before I looked closely enough to realize what had happened. The blades are small, and it can be hard to notice flaws if you aren't looking. But you can avoid damage to your blades by caring for them appropriately. When not in use, store your blades properly, especially if you keep them in a go bag. I believe my favorite blade got bent when I was lazy and just tossed it into my go bag without tucking it safely away in the container first. Even if you are using inexpensive tools, it is important to treat them with respect so you can continue to create flawless artwork.

Pay Attention to Blade Depth

We already discussed carving depth in an earlier lesson, but we are going to come back to that for a moment, because it is one of my top tips for achieving clean cuts. Eraser rubber is incredibly soft, and it can be easy to dig too deeply with your carving blades. If you are using a blade with a shallower shape, it is possible to accidentally carve so deep into the eraser that the top corners of your blade slip below the surface of the eraser. If this happens, those blade corners will shred your eraser, causing messy cuts. It is important to take notice of the blade as you carve to ensure this does not happen.

Carve with Confidence

I find that one of the best ways to achieve a clean cut is to create that cut with confidence. Moving with an even speed through a cut will be one of the most effective ways to create clean, bold lines. Eraser rubber is so soft that hesitation will show in your lines. It is also true that going too slowly allows more opportunity to cause a wiggle in your lines. This doesn't mean that you should speed through your carving, but rather to choose a line and follow it through with even speed and confidence.

Don't Overwork It

If you find yourself with some shredded cut edges, running multiple times over a cut line in an attempt to clean it up can actually make it worse. You can clean up a cut line if you are willing to remove quite a bit of eraser from the area, but doing a quick skim over your cut in an attempt to shave off a shredded bit will often just push the shredded bits around or make them worse.

Perfection Takes Time

If you find yourself with shredded edges on a piece, don't give up. Remember that practice helps you grow, and spending time with the medium will enable you to figure out the finesse that you need to create your tiny art. You might find that you are teaching yourself fine motor skills that you haven't called on before, and it can take time practicing the craft to improve those skills. Don't forget that the best part of working with erasers is that it is a low-cost and low-risk medium, and you can afford to make terrible art in order to make great art later on.

Tip

Don't throw away your shredded or ruined eraser art pieces! There are six sides on every eraser, and you can use all of those sides to practice technique or to try your art piece again. It is also good to have scrap erasers on hand for when you are sharpening your blades and need to do test cuts. You don't need to save everything, but it is good practice to use the material to its fullest before tossing it in the trash.

11

Marks and Lines

Printmaking at its core is based in working with only two values (negative and positive space) or, more simply, two shades of color (black and white). When we draw with graphite or paint with watercolor, we can build layers to create an endless variety of values. You can create many layers with printmaking as well when using a variety of colored inks (we will get into that later in the book). For now, we are recognizing that the primary nature of a single print is that with one stamp there are only two values. And so, we have the challenge of creating the illusion of color shades, and we do that with hatch marks.

Using Hatch Marks for Value Gradient

Hatch mark shading is a foundational drawing technique and is essential in printmaking.

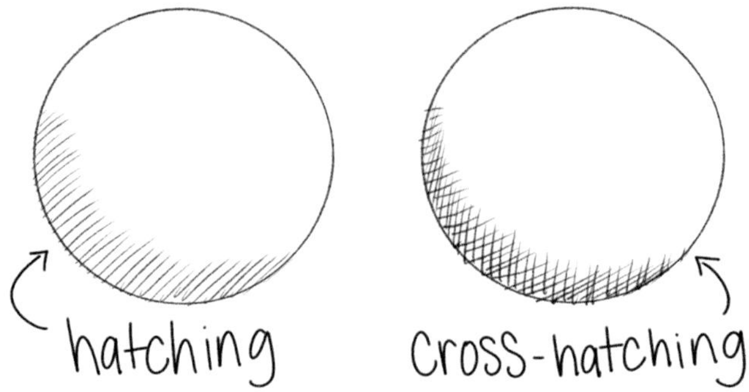

While we can't turn our blade on its side and create shading like we could with a charcoal pencil, we can carve a whole bunch of little lines. There are a few tricks to using hatch mark shading to create the illusion of various values. Remember that you are carving your hatch marks away, so every cut will be negative space. The amount of space you leave between your hatch marks will create the illusion of various values. You can control this by making your hatch marks closer together or farther apart by the thickness of your hatch marks or by adding cross-hatching. Cross-hatching is done by carving perpendicular lines on top of your hatch marks, which makes crosses and can create value as well as texture.

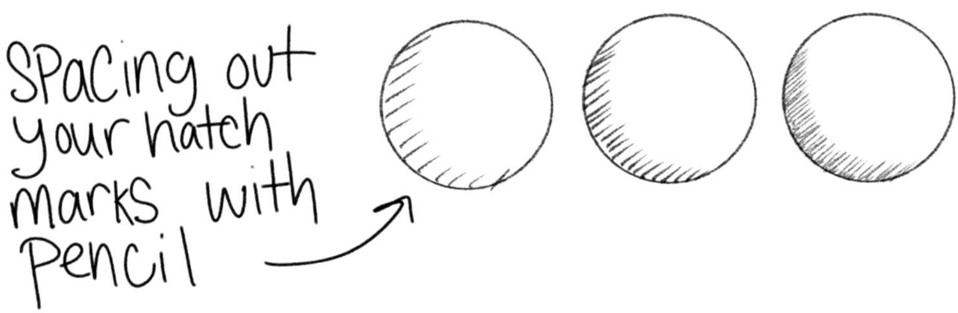

In this Volkswagen bus piece, I used a couple of hatch marks to create the reflection on the windshield.

In this conchas piece, I brought light into the shadow areas at the bottom of the pan dulces with cross-hatching.

In this mountains piece, I used the most straightforward hatching method to add value and shadow to the mountains.

In this peony piece, I used lines to make the flower petals, creating the shapes with positive and negative space guided by the lines.

In this chips and guacamole piece, I brought highlights and texture into the molcajete with mini hatch lines.

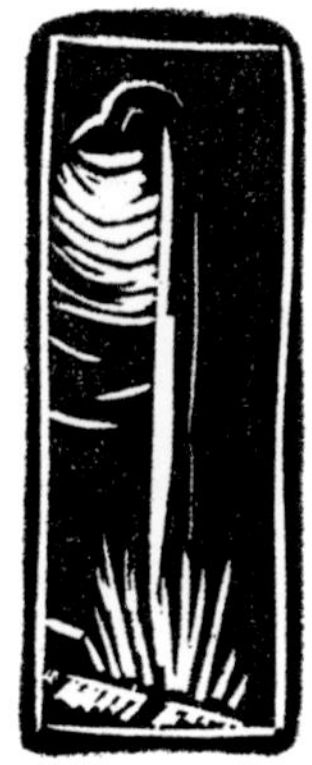

In this streetlamp piece, I used curved lines in a gradient to create the illusion of shining light.

In this braid piece, I used curved hatch lines to add highlights to the hair.

In this piece, I used my most complex attempt at hatch marks to create the softness of light shining on rumpled sheets.

Using Carve Lines to Create Texture and Movement

I am unashamed to admit that I am obsessive about the cleanliness of my prints. I spend additional time carving down the negative spaces on my erasers to ensure that no matter how hard I stamp or how soft my paper, nothing will transfer ink onto my print unless I mean it to. That is why I was blown away when I realized that not only do many printmakers allow their carve lines to make it to print but deliberately shape them to assist in the story they are telling with their artwork. When I saw this deliberate shaping of negative spaces used effectively for the first time my jaw did actually drop open, and my mind was effectively blown.

My signature style is graphic, bold, and clean; it never occurred to me to use the carve lines as a tool for expression. Sharing this with you is important because it illustrates the importance of viewing others' artwork and shows how people can do wildly diverse things with the same tools. It reiterates the idea I previously shared that we should never limit our subject choices because someone else already used it. Our diverse backgrounds, preferences, and skills cause us to create many different types of flowers, for example, that can inspire people in different ways. And the world needs that.

Generally, when I carve, my goal is only to remove the negative spaces effectively and do so while creating clean, crisp lines and shapes. So, the direction of my cuts and how I move my blade is focused solely on one thing: the lines forming the positive spaces. It is simple and easy and I like it. When I carve, I only use the foremost layer to tell any story or create any movement. If there is a ripple, or the light is shining in a particular direction, it is part of my design and carving that directional movement is part of the planned image.

However, we can allow the accidental printed lines that happen when we press too hard on our eraser to enter the chat, and when we do, it can have absolutely breathtaking effects. The first time I saw a linoleum carving printed in this way I was reminded of the Post-Impressionists' beloved paintings, such as Vincent van Gough's *Starry Night* and Edvard Munch's *The Scream*, but created entirely with a single-color value, all with the use of the carving blade.

This style of carving adds a second technique. We are no longer solely focused on creating clean lines but also need to make our cuts with intention, even in the negative spaces. It's similar to coloring in a coloring book. When you near the edges of the image, you pay more attention to the motions you make as you fill in the spaces with ink. Scribbly coloring will make scribbly marker lines. If you want a uniform look, you will color in straight lines, right? Or maybe you follow the curves in the artwork, but, knowing that your marker will leave lines in the inked areas, you are intentional with the lines you use to fill the space.

This concept can be used in eraser carving, but with the marks we leave behind as we remove material from our carving.

Depending on your design, the carve lines can happen naturally or may be something you plan out. Remember, the deeper you carve into the eraser's negative space the less likely the carve lines are to print, so this technique is best achieved on the first pass. It is something to have in mind as you create the initial carving, not something you can create after the fact.

Tapering Your Lines

Carving into something as soft as an eraser is cool because we have so much control over how we use our carving blade. Let's talk about tapering our lines. I feel extra nerdy about this one because the concept is the same as when I taught watercolor workshops and brush technique! I really love it when artistic techniques intersect across art mediums. It is proof that taking time to do silly little art mediums, like carving stamps out of erasers, does teach you real skills you can use in many other ways. Don't let anyone make you believe that you aren't making "real art" if you are using odd materials instead of classic mediums and professional brands! I am about to teach you a technique that is also used in watercolor, brush lettering, and classic calligraphy: creating a delicately tapered line.

What is a tapered line and how do we make one? A tapered line is when the width of a line slowly thins and ends with a point. Tapered lines can be curved or straight. They can be how you finish off a word in cursive, or they can be details in a flower petal. When I taught watercolor painting, we used tapered lines to create the thin petals of daisies, and it is all in the pressure of the brush stroke. The same rule applies when carving. You will need to use the V-shaped blade to create a tapered point; you can explore creating tapered lines with any size V-shaped blade. A larger V-shaped blade will allow you to make thicker lines, but because it is still shaped like a v, no matter how big the blade is, you should still be able to carve it out to a perfect point.

How to Make a Tapered Line End in a Point

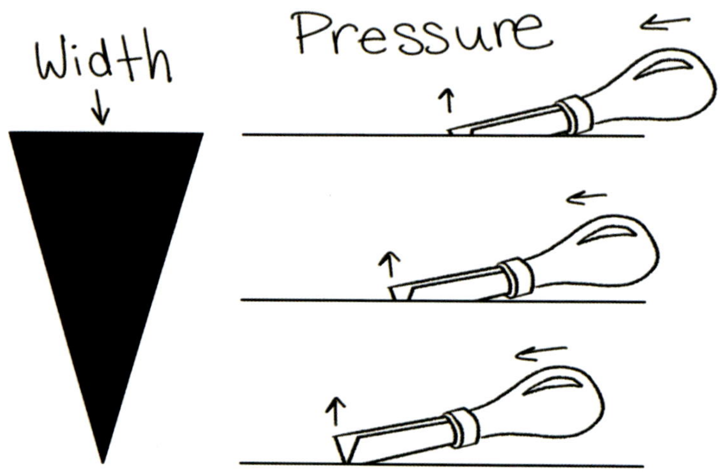

Begin carving your line with your V-shaped blade using a fair bit of pressure to cut deeply into the eraser surface, which will create a wide line.

Continue to carve your line while releasing pressure on the blade until you eventually raise it out and away from the eraser surface entirely, creating a point.

How to Make a Tapered Line Start with a Point

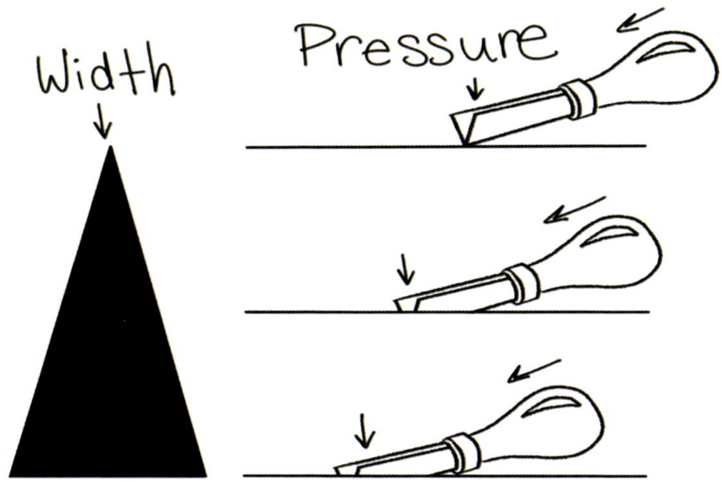

Begin carving your line with the blade barely scraping the surface, keeping the blade parallel to the eraser surface.

As you carve your line, gradually add pressure, so the blade dips deeper into the eraser.

When you reach the end of the line, lift the blade straight up out of the eraser to cut off the line. Slowly release pressure from the blade as you carve forward until the blade eventually raises from the surface, creating a point.

Making Marks with Unusual Tools

As in all art practices, your carving blade is not your only tool. When it comes to any type of mark making, whether you are creating with paints or carving away sides of rubber erasers, you are only limited by your imagination. Look around your space and see if there is anything else you can press into your eraser. Try it (this is why we never throw scrapped erasers away!) and see what type of marks you can make! When you experiment with new mark-making tools, remember to be careful, because if you find something that can cut through your eraser, there is every chance it may also cut through you. Be mindful, take care, and have fun experimenting and exploring. You may find that pushing yourself to see tools in a new way will spark another level of creativity and imagination.

Alternate Tools to Try

Ballpoint pens
Thumbtacks
Paper clips
Marker caps
Skewers
Forks
Precision engraving tools
The ferrule of a broken paint brush, or a pencil that lost its eraser

Activity: Practice Tapering

Tapering your lines and creating texture with your carve lines is one of my favorite parts of carving flower petals, leaves, and vines. Plants have so much variety in color, which is why people love to paint them, but they are also rich in shape and texture, which makes them so much fun to carve. Here are a few shapes that you can practice creating with your blade. Play with shape and width and getting those tapered ends sharp and clean. You can allow your carve lines to show as you do this, which will add a natural texture to your leaves and petals.

Other Ideas

Explore your home, kitchen, or office and look for objects you think could make interesting marks. Press them into your eraser and see what happens. What do the unusual marks inspire you to create? How do you feel after exploring odd tools and stabbing your eraser a little? I'll bet you feel a little bit better than you did when you started.

12

Spacing Out Letters

The first time I decided to carve letters onto an eraser I intuited the method without really thinking. Later, I realized that I had based my method on a street artist I watched in Mexico about fourteen years prior. As I carved out words for the first time, I didn't remember watching the artist work as he carved, "Mi amor" into a key, but somehow recalled the method he used to do it. To me, this is proof that not only does street art and performance have so much value as we connect as humans but taking the time to watch and support the arts benefits us as much as the artists.

This method of mapping out words on your eraser surface is a way to make them bold and perfectly spaced. I do this, rather than transfer the words with a graphite rubbing, when I want everything placed precisely within the border of my eraser. With rubbing transfers, there is always the risk that the slightest shift will set every line slightly off kilter, and so, this is the most precise way to get every letter exactly like you want it.

Carving Words

1. The first step is to plan out what you want to write. If you have more than one word, you will need to plan how to stack them. If you are carving a single word, like a name, you get to make it big and bold and take up the entire space. If you are carving two words, you will stack one on top of the other. If you are carving three or more words, you'll want to put either two on top and one on bottom, or vice versa, based on how they fit.

2. Write out your words backward. If this is difficult for you, simply write the words on a piece of paper, flip it over, and then hold it up to the light, trace the letters, and then you will have the mirror image of your word to copy from. It is essential that your word and letters are all carved in their mirror image, otherwise they will be backward when you print. If this is still difficult for you, that's okay, it's perfectly normal. I made a cheat sheet for you with the alphabet in upper and lowercase letters. Practice writing backward, checking your work by holding your paper up to the light. If you can read the words and letters correctly from the back of the page, you did it!

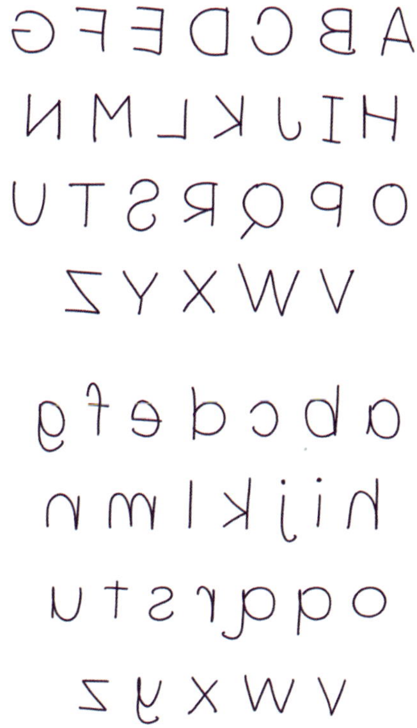

3. Find the center of your word and mark it. If the word you are carving has an even number of letters, the center of the word is the space between the center-most letters. If the word has an odd number of letters, the center of the word is the middle letter. For example, “eraser” is six letters, so the center is the space between the letters A and S. “Art” is three letters, so the center of the word is the center of the letter R.

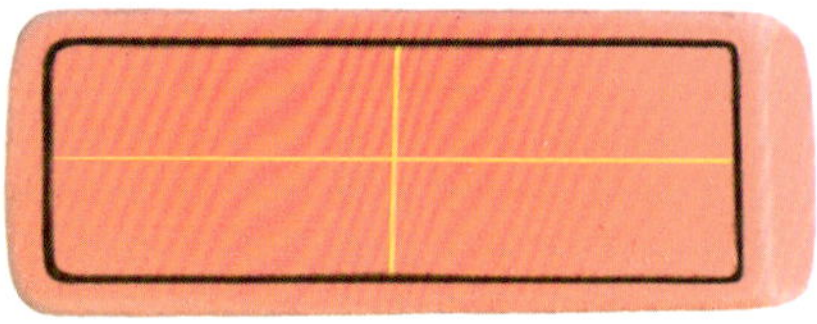

4. Mark the center of the eraser. This does not need to be precise, so you can simply eyeball the center of the eraser and draw a line down the middle. If you are stacking more than one word, draw a second line across the middle of the eraser from left to right.

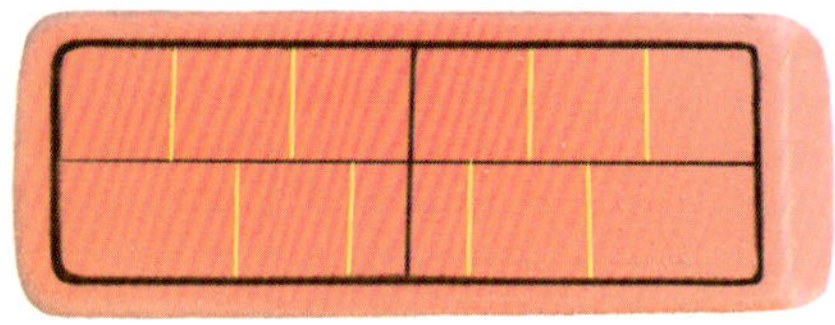

5. Mark out spaces for each letter evenly to the left and right of your center mark. If your word has an even number of letters, you will count your center mark as a space between the letters. If your word has an odd number of letters, the center mark will be the center of your middle letter and you will need to mark a space on both sides of the center letter as well. After you have your spaces marked evenly across your eraser, use those marks to draw a line from top to bottom.

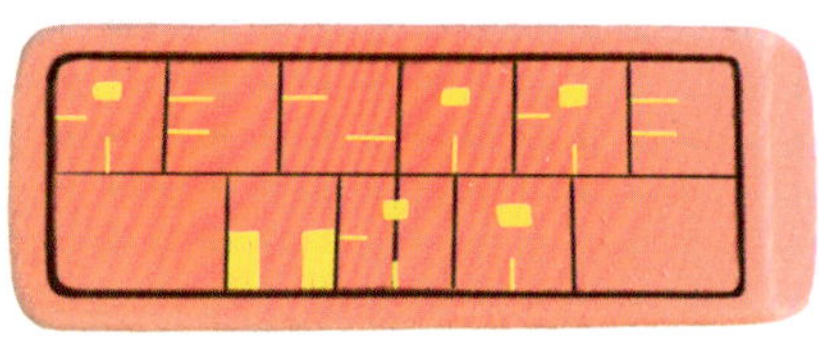

6. Draw your letters. Use lines to mark the shape of your letters. Remember to mark them to create the letters as a mirror image of themselves.

7. Carve over your drawn lines.

Carving Your Letters

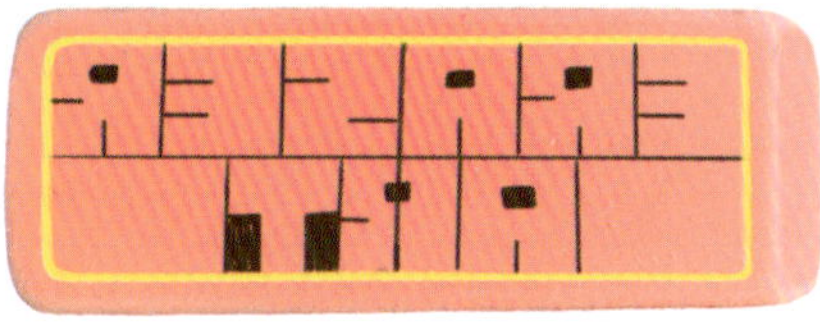

1. Start with your border line.

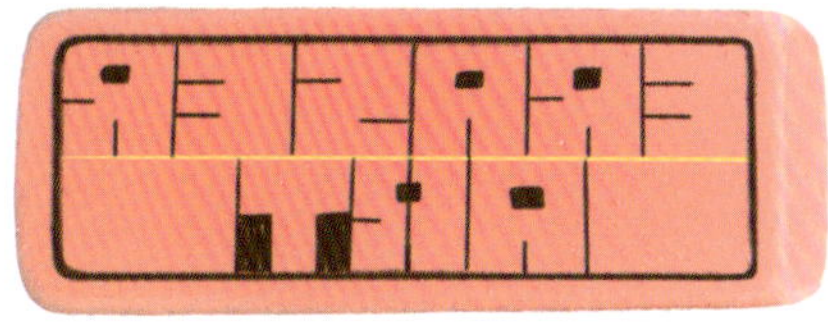

2. Carve the horizontal line if you have two rows of words.

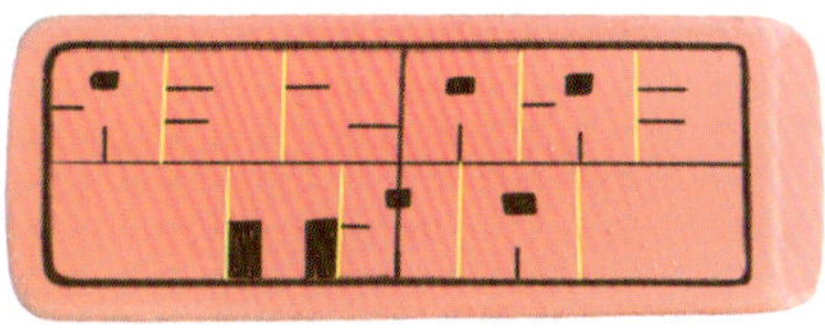

3. Carve out the vertical spaces between the letters.

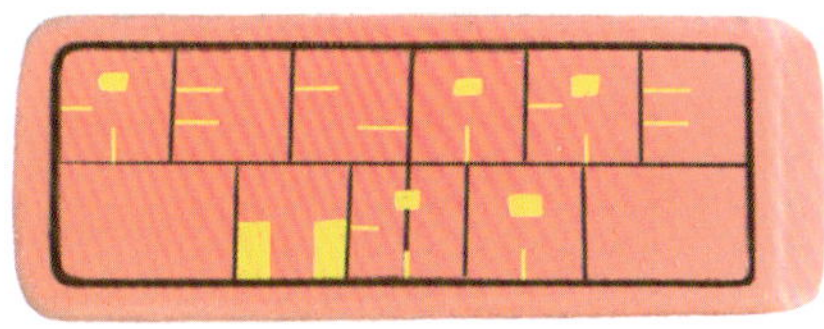

4. Carve the lines and dashes that will create the shapes of your bold block letters.

5. If you want to round off your letters, carve around the corners.

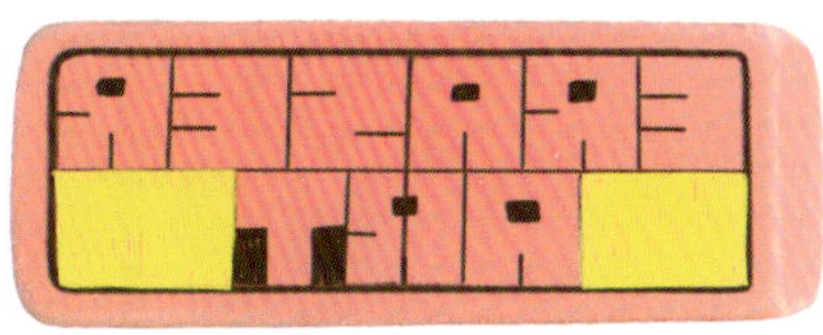

6. Carve out any unused space.

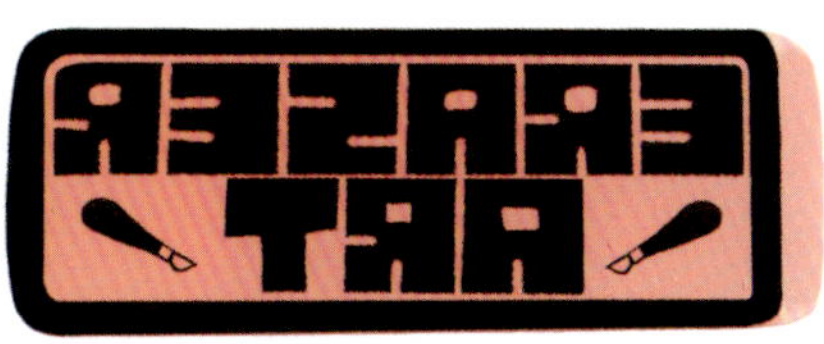

7. Ink your eraser.

8. Stamp it!

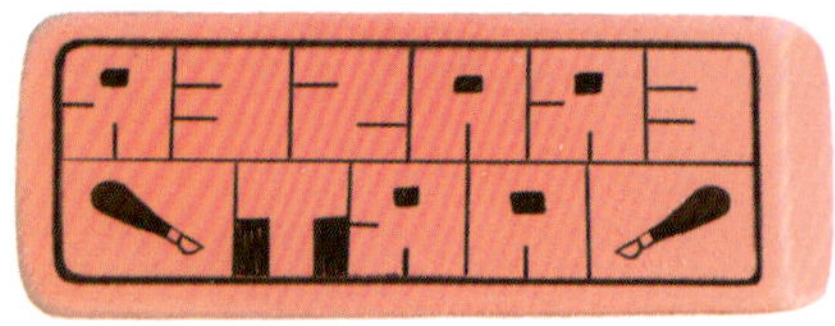

Tip

You can add art to any empty spaces!

You can leave your block letters chunky and square, or you can go over your lines again to carve them out thicker, making your letters slightly smaller. You may also play around with rounding off the corners of your letters or adjusting the shape in whatever fun ways you want.

Alphabet Carving Guide

Take note that there are some tricky letters in our alphabet because they are similar but reversed or flipped. The most difficult letters to get right are d, b, p, and q. N, Z, S, and 5 can also be tricky while mirroring and carving. Use the light-ray method to double-check your letters before you start your sketch.

PINK
ERASER
ART

13

Circles, Curves, and Cursive

Carving smooth curves is one of the most soothing and satisfying ways to carve into the soft rubber of erasers, and when I find myself carving a design with a lot of curves it feels as if I'm cruising down a winding mountain highway. I love it. The technique I have established to successfully carve curves into these tiny erasers uses both hands in tandem, and when you master it, it is all vibes. It feels like meditation. When we use our hands to create, we are connecting our mind and body to the present moment, and when we use both hands in motion together to create, it brings us fully into the present moment.

Carving smooth, flawless curves can be difficult because it needs to be done with confident motion and no hesitation. This is one of those situations where every pause will become a visible part of your art piece. Go into this lesson with fearless confidence! And let me make this important note: no hesitation does not mean fast, it means to be steady and consistent.

Carving Curves

To carve the smoothest curved lines without any nicks or angles, you will be moving both hands at once. While directing your blade with your carving hand, turn the eraser into the blade with your other hand. To accomplish this smoothly, apply equal pressure with both actions, pushing the blade and the eraser into each other, while following the curved line of your sketch with a rotating motion.

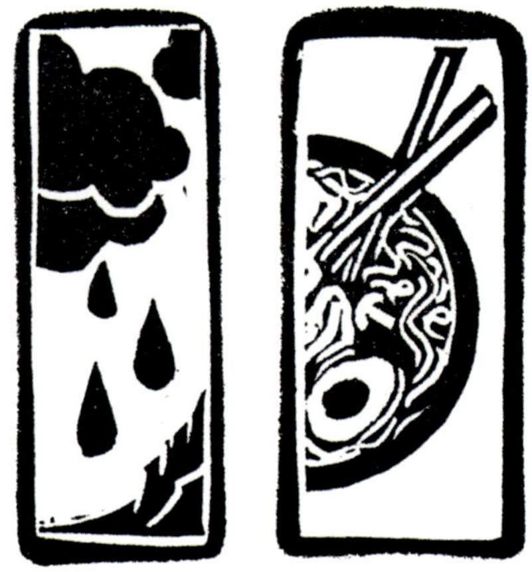

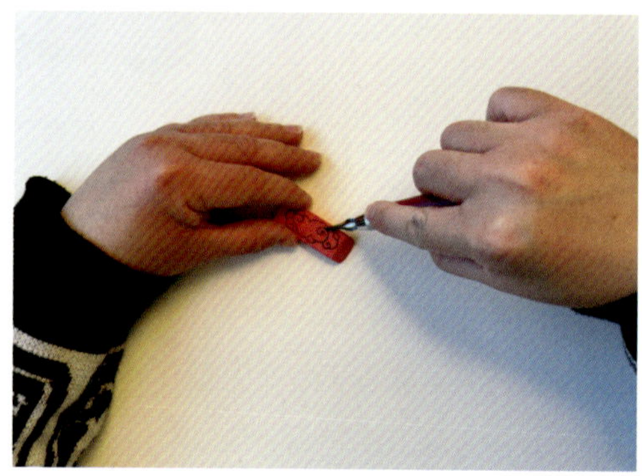

The goal is to make the full line of a curve with one cut. If you try to carve a curved line with several smaller cuts, you will likely achieve a more jagged edge, with inconsistencies in your curve. This happens because some cuts may be straighter than others, and where you begin the cut again you will likely see a joint, because it can be difficult to pick up carving exactly where you left off. Consistent results require consistent actions.

This technique can create smooth curves of any size, whether they are large and arcing across the whole eraser surface, or tiny like the rounded center of a letter. The difference is simply the swiftness with which you rotate the eraser as you carve. A quick rotation with a small cut will create small curves—even small circles or dots if needed, if you carry the eraser rotations through a full 360°. A slower rotation with a longer cut will create larger arcs and curves.

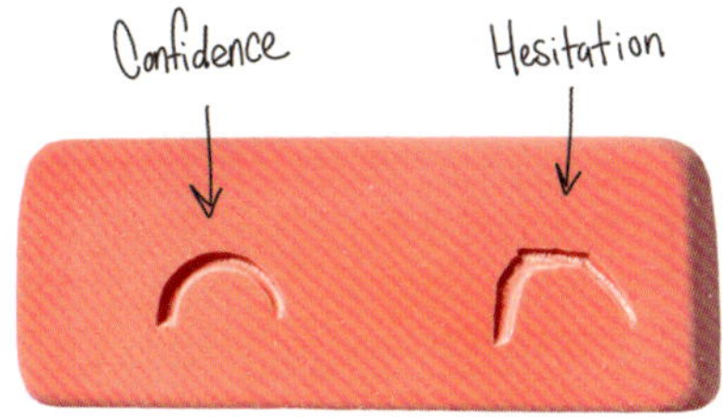

Cursive

Carving line-drawing style over cursive lettering is a great way to practice your curves at different widths and angles. Try transferring your signature onto your eraser to carve, or create name stamps for your friends! You can also practice by making day-of-the-week stamps or month stamps to use in your planner, bullet journal, or junk journal, DON'T FORGET: All words must be carved onto your eraser backward in order to be printed forward. All carvings are a mirror image of the desired print.

Circles

Carving the tiniest circles is easily my favorite thing to do; I love adding circles, dots, or bubbles into my designs just to be able to do it more.

Carving a Tiny Circle

1. Set your carving blade onto the eraser, pressing the blade straight down.
2. Holding your blade in place, rotate the eraser a full 360°.

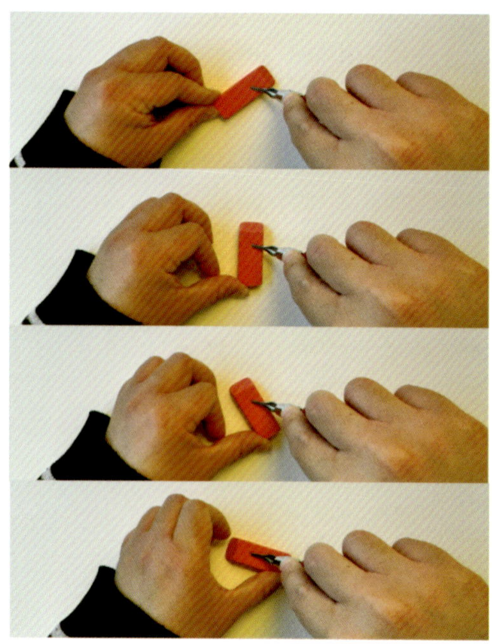

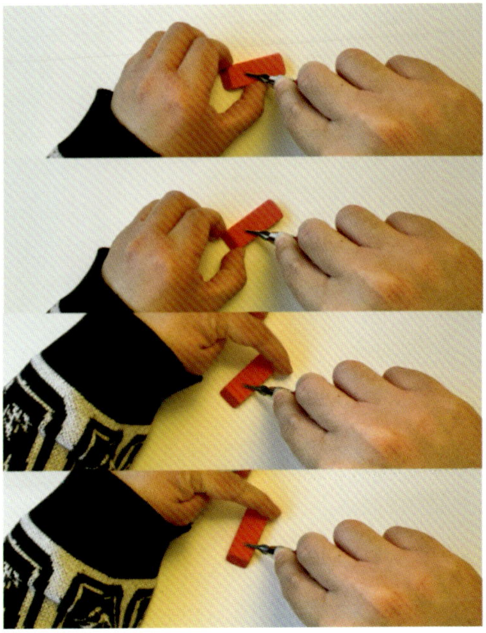

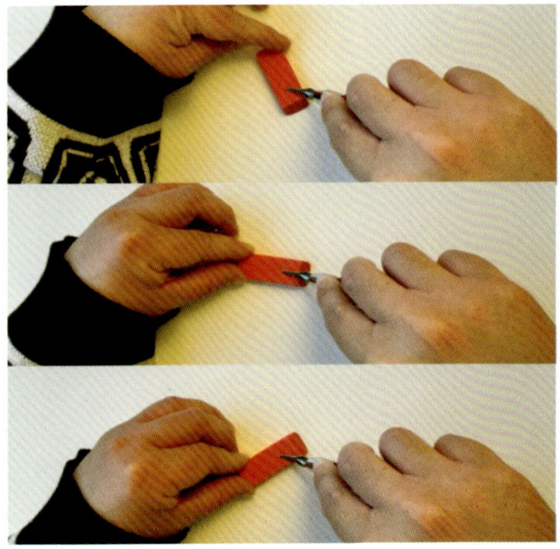

3. Lift your carving blade straight up to reveal your tiny circle.

Tip

If your circle doesn't come out even, and has a weird little angle, rotate your blade outward while carving your tiny circle to line the cut up on the return.

Activity: Kawaii Face Stamp

Easily one of my favorite stamps of all time is this little face I made one time. I want to stamp it on everything. I want to stamp it on still life photographs in my junk journal. I want to make a new version of the *Mona Lisa*. I want to make everything I come across in coupons and junk mail a little bit happier. The possibilities are endless, and the desire to interact with the world around me is enhanced with this eraser. You can make a lot of different types of faces, but this little guy is perfect for practicing tiny curves and circles.

1. Because we are carving away the border, this face does not need to be measured perfectly into the center. But if you want to center it, eyeball the centerline, mark it, and start by drawing the little smile.

2. Draw two big circles for the eyes with two little circles inside the eyes to create highlights.

3. Little blushed cheeks make everything more adorable, so now draw a small, horizontal oval to the outside of each eye.

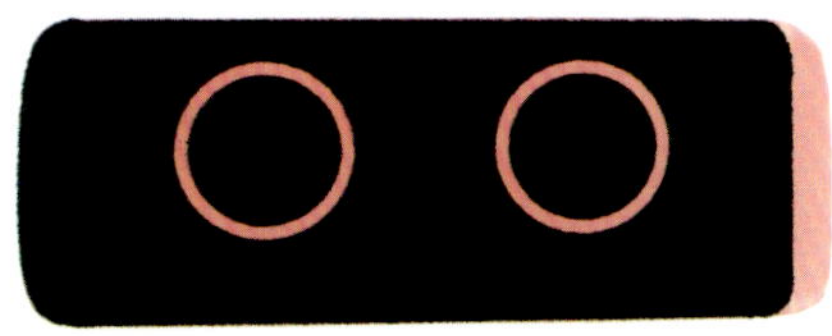

4. Carve the outline of your eyes first because they are the focal point, and you want them to be as clean as possible.

5. Use the tiniest circle trick to carve the smallest possible circles inside the eye to create highlights.

6. Carve around the mouth shape.

7. Carve out the oval cheeks by first carving the outside and then gently hollowing out the center of the shape. Use a 180° turn for each of the oval ends.

8. Carve out the rest of the eraser, smoothing down the carve lines for the cleanest stamp possible.

14

Carving Those Tiny Details

We've talked about how to carve sweeping, elegant curves, now let's talk about the staccato of the carve—the tiniest details of all—and how to create them. Removing the smallest pieces of the eraser surface while still creating delicate angles and lines can be done. These details always arrive in my artwork on accident, and I hate it every time. As I design my artwork, I often sketch out a line drawing before I even think about the positive and negative space. And while creating any artwork with the intention to carve out the lines is easy, choosing to carve out around the lines is intricate and requires careful and thoughtful carving. I do often hate it the entire time I am carving, but each time it has been worth the meticulous precision and emotional turmoil, and I am always glad I took the time to try something so delicate that I wasn't even sure I could pull it off at all. I'm here to tell you that you can absolutely carve smaller and more precise than you think possible.

When to Carve Tiny Angles

There are lines and angles everywhere in our lives, and it is easy not to pay attention until you decide to re-create something with art. That is why I always end up with intensely detailed sketches without realizing what I am signing up for. Let's think about some details that might come up in precision drawings: the squares inside a waffle, windows on a skyscraper or in a bus, points on a star, parking lights, or the diced veggies in pico de gallo. None of these are too daunting, until we shrink them down to fit inside a one-inch eraser. Once it is shrunk down to size, the windows on a skyscraper are so tiny! And repetitive. And square. How do we create the tiniest squares with our tiny blades?

How to Carve Tiny Angles

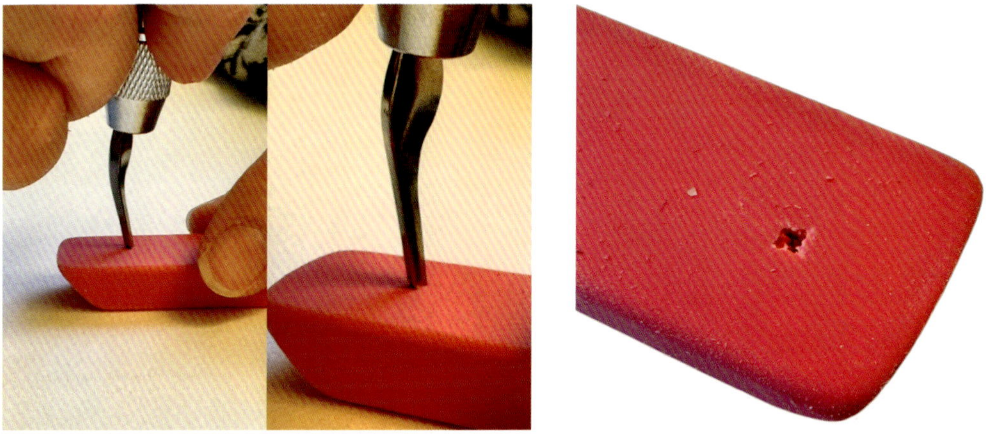

STAB IT! But carefully. At the beginning of this book, I taught you to carve with your blade parallel to the eraser, but now is one of those moments where I break my own rule. Let's go! Take a second to stare down your carving blade like it is high noon in the Old West. Look at it straight on and notice the angle of the V-blade. That is going to be the corner of your squares or the point of an angle you need to create. Use the smallest V-blade in your carving set. In order to capture that tiny shape, turn your carving tool perpendicular to your eraser—a 90° angle—and place it on top of where you need that angle to be. Press it down into the eraser, making a cut exactly on the corner of your tiny shape. If your shape has more corners, do the same action around each of them before carefully scooping out the material in the center.

Ending a Line with a Straight Edge

If you have to create a sharp angle at the end of a shape or line you are carving toward, it is even easier. Holding your carving tool parallel to the eraser, carve along your desired line until you reach all the way to the end, and then lift your blade straight out of the eraser at a 90° angle. This isn't something you can pull off with hard material, such as linoleum, but the rubber of erasers is so soft that when you lift your blade out, it will simply break off the piece you have carved and create a straight line and clear angle every time. If you are nervous about the rubber shifting or tearing, you can hold it in the nook of the blade with your forefinger as you lift the blade away, causing a clean break.

TIP: The smaller the details, the more stubborn the eraser can be about releasing the pieces you are carving away. When you have tiny bits that are difficult to carve out, use your fingertip. Place your fingertip on the stubborn area you need to clean up and rub the surface in a circular motion. The friction from your fingertip should gently tear away the tiny pieces you are trying to remove without affecting your carving design.

Tip

When cleaning up any stray little pieces of eraser you missed during the carving process, you can use the same technique of coming in with the blade at a 90° angle if you need to remove it carefully.

Activity: Checkerboard

I find itty-bitty boxes and corners to be the most difficult and tedious of the tiny details. The perfect way to practice is to make a lot of them. Let's create a checkerboard: it is so simple to draw, and the perfect practice for carving out tiny edges, lines, and corners!

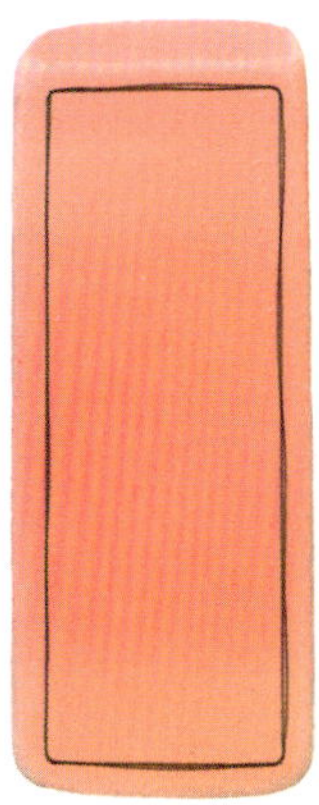

1. Sketch your border, if you are using one.

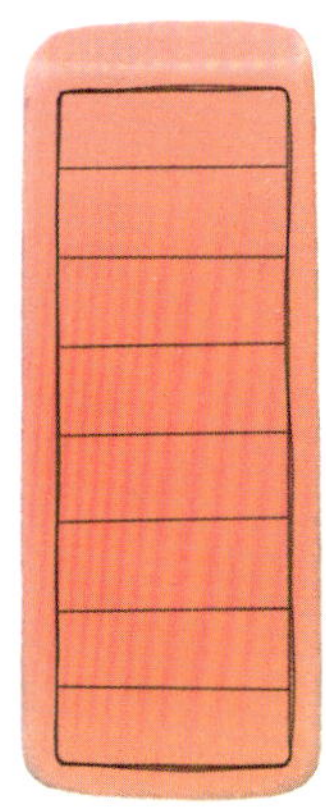

2. Draw horizontal lines across your eraser.

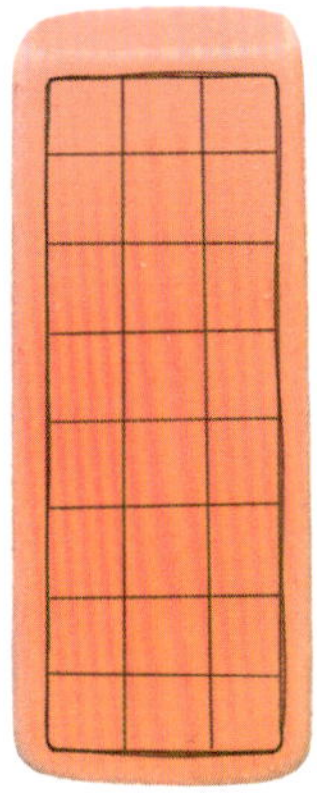

3. Draw vertical lines across your eraser.

4. Color in every other square.

5. Carve out the negative spaces, practicing what you learned in this section!

Challenge: Do this activity with a wobbly checkerboard design.

15

Creating Drama with Lighting

I took my very first art class in sixth grade, and I don't remember a single thing except this: plan the direction of your light source before you begin your drawing. Light is an essential part of seeing anything in the world. It is part of how our brains process the passage of time. Think about how we do that. How does looking out a window help us determine if it is time for a little treat, yet? It is the observation of light and shadow. That's why time feels confusing on a cloudy or rainy day. Because whether we realize it or not, we use the direction of the sun and the shape of shadows to navigate ourselves through the day. Now let's head inside. We still require light indoors; throughout your home, studio, office, or classroom you have different light sources—windows, lamps, fluorescent ceiling lights, decorative neon wall lights, and soft, ambient lights. Lighting options are endless and have a strong influence on the ambience of a space, and our behavior within that space.

Gentle, soft lighting helps us feel calm and cozy. Strong, dramatic lighting makes a statement and probably makes us want to wear our sparkliest eyeshadow, because drama! Ambient lighting has less impact, while strong, directional light emphasizes shape and form.

Because we are working with only two values, black and white, we can have fun with lighting in our designs. We can literally draw the lines of a spotlight, making a dramatic shadow with just a simple curve. We can make a thick carved line to create moonlight. I have so much fun creating eraser carvings that show the form of a shape by cutting out only the highlights of a strong directional light. Playing with light sources in relief carving can become an entire exploration in itself, and it is incredibly fun.

Determining Your Light Source

After you have made your sketch, it is time to decide where you want your light source to be. Generally, my light sources come from above, often marked to the upper left, right, or center of the eraser, but depending on your design, the light source can come from anywhere (remember the flashlight trick, while telling scary stories to your friends as a kid?). If you are creating a tiny piece of art and you want the drama, this is how to make it.

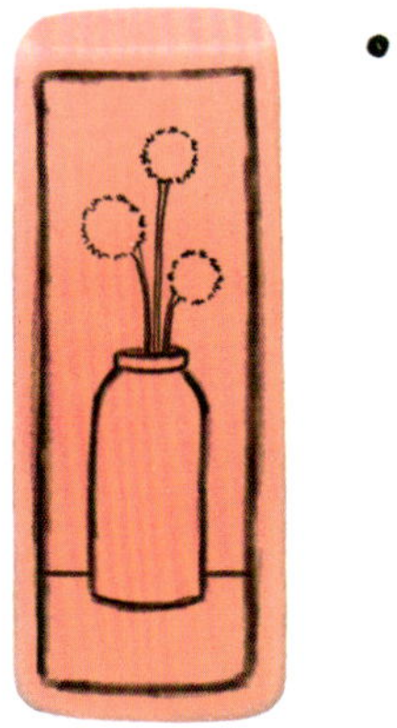

1. Choose where your light source is and mark it with a dot.

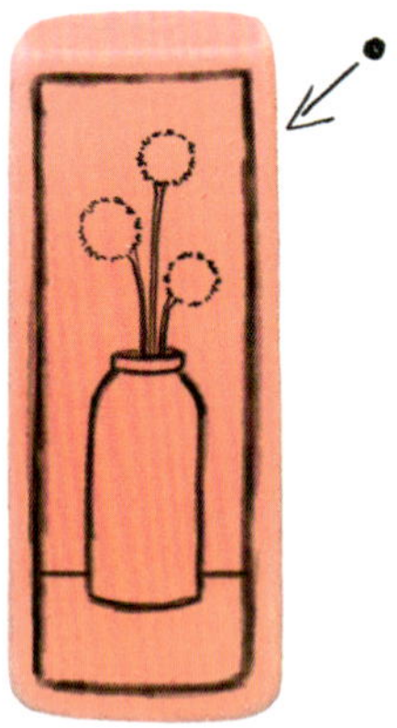

2. Draw a little arrow pointing in the direction it is shining from the dot.

3. Identify your objects in the sketch and determine the highlights and shadows.

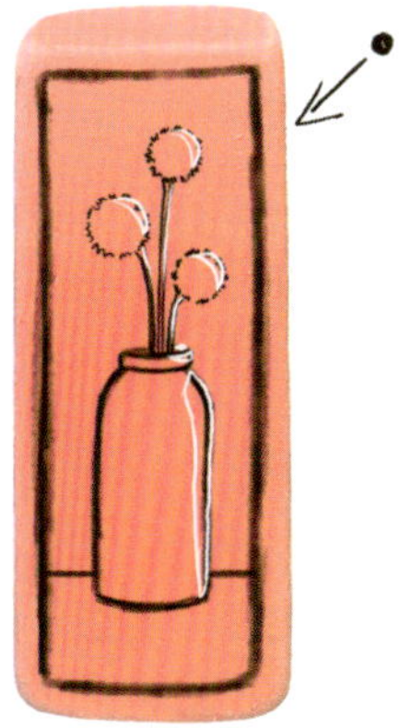

3a. Highlights will be on the side closest to the arrow.

3b. Shadows will be on the side farthest from the arrow.

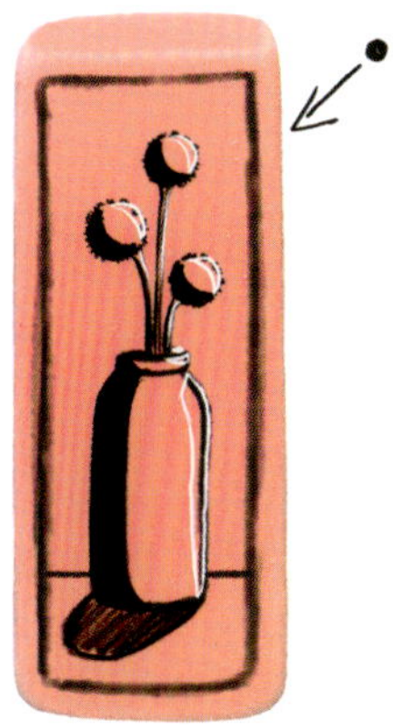

4. Draw the shadow cast from your subject. This shadow will follow the same direction as the arrow, from the base of your subject.

Tip

The shadow can be created with hatch marks or a bold, positive-space shape.

Creating Art with a Strong, Directional Light Source

It is so fun to create pictures and objects while carving out every little detail, and that's what I did more than one hundred times with this art medium before I began to explore something new. I carved an orange blossom, and I carved out only the highlights. Anything that was in shadow stayed in shadow. This is one of my favorite styles of photography, and attempting the same dramatic studio lighting on a tiny eraser brought me a lot of joy. In order to carve in this way, I had to think of each of the highlights as its own shape, and when I carved out this arrangement of odd shapes, they created a larger image. It is like a fun puzzle.

In studio photography, you begin planning your lighting arrangement with a key light, or your main light source. It was my favorite thing to use only this single light to create photographs like the image we just discussed. But sometimes I wanted to bring a little bit more shape into the image. Instead of bringing in a second light, I would just use a big, white, board to reflect the key light back onto the other side of my subject. This would cause a very soft outline of the subject to emerge from the darkness.

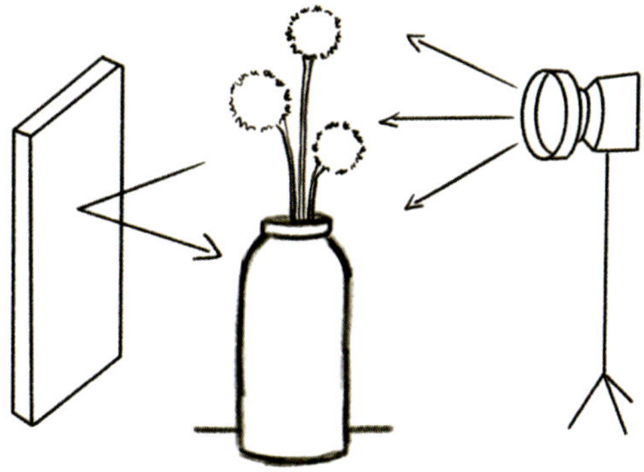

We can do the same thing in printmaking. First, we determine the light source and then we carve out our large, dramatic highlights.

Next, we bring in that reflective light source by carving out the shape of our subject with a thin line-drawing-style carve in the shadowy half of the image.

You can explore playing with shapes and lighting in this way, and if you can't decide if you want to add more detail or not, you can always pause and do a test print onto paper before you continue carving. If you love it, you're done, and if you want more detail, just wash off your eraser and continue carving out that detail.

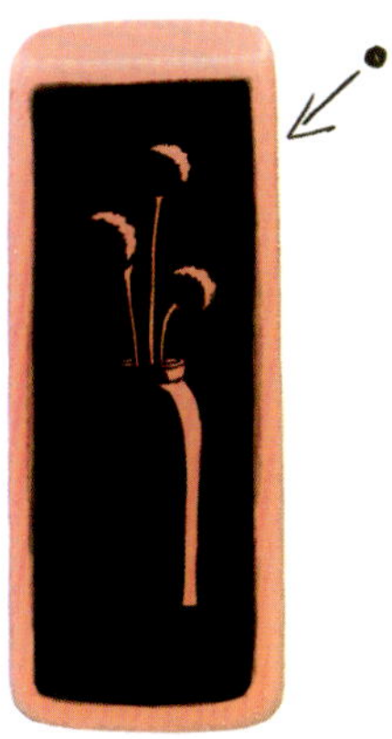

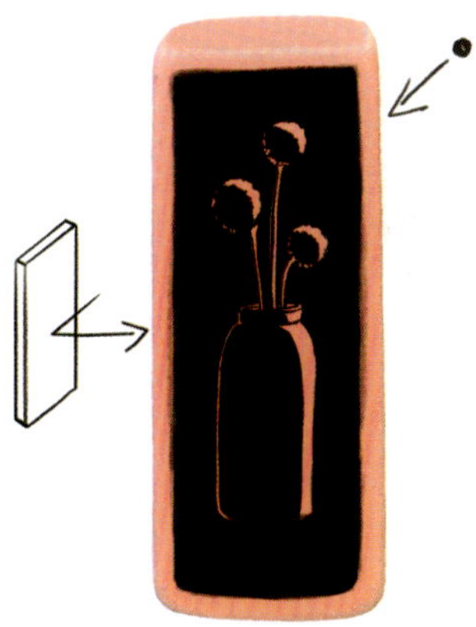

When Your Light Source Is in the Frame

There are so many designs that can invite the source of light directly into the frame, like streetlights, flashlights, matches, and candles, but I think the moon is my favorite so far. We can look directly at her, unlike the sun, and so humans have drawn and painted the moon for as long as we have been creating art. The moon is one of the gentlest sources of soft, ambient light. The moon is also a great starting point when you are trying to decide your positive and negative space, asking yourself what you should carve away and what you should leave behind. Why? Because when your source of light is in the design, it will always be the first thing you carve away. Every time I have created an eraser carving with the moon she is always the first thing I carve out, and everything else follows. Here are the steps:

1. Carve out the shape and details of your light source.
2. Identify the shapes around the light source and carve out the highlights on the sides closest to it. Carve these lines out a bit thicker and wider and shape the highlights to emphasize the shape of the objects.

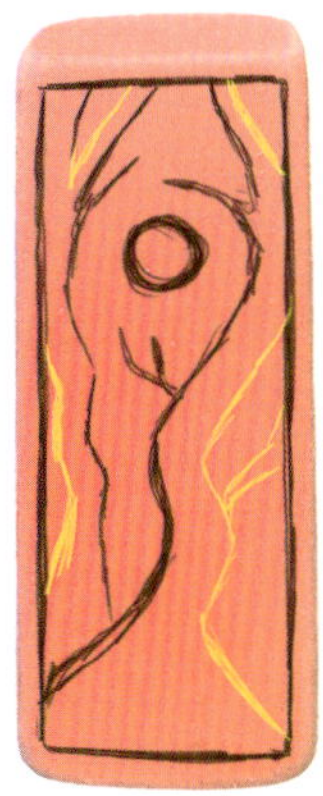

3. Carve out thin detail lines on the opposite side of the objects, if you want, to bring detail and shape into the shadows.

4. Ink the stamp.

Emphasizing Little Highlights

When I was a child, I was obsessed with drawing heart balloons, and I thought I was really cool because I knew how to make a shaped highlight that made the balloons look 3D.

I was a whole artist, and I knew it! I have brought that idea into my eraser carvings, and it creates an effect that makes me feel as cool as I did drawing those 3D highlights on my ballon sketches as a kid. It might seem silly to carve a highlight in an already highlighted area, but I love it, and so I'm going to show you how to do it too. Think about when you see the sun shining on a vase or a car. There are lots of illuminated shapes and highlights across the surface, but there's always that one point right in the center that is just a wholly white, bright reflection of the sun itself. I use an outline, like the one in my childhood drawings, to express that brightest point in the sun's reflected light. It is a little bit cartoony, but brings in the feeling of a direct, bright light, rather than a gentle, ambient one.

Carving Highlights

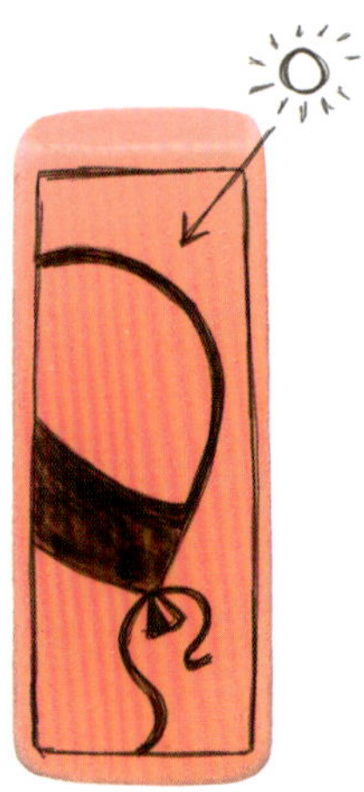

1. Determine the direction of your light source and color in the shadows, leaving the highlighted area open.

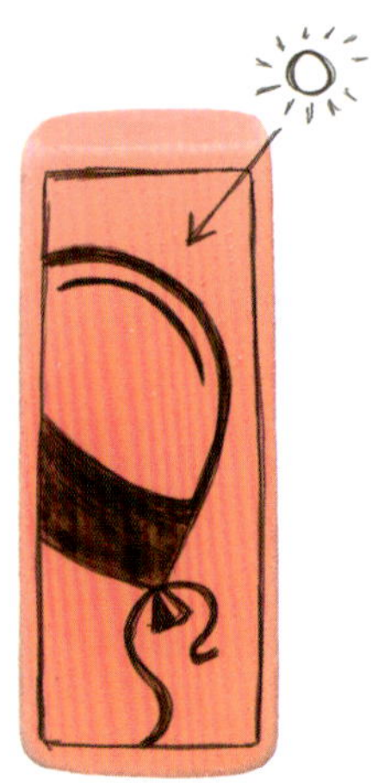

2. Draw a line that follows the shape of your subject nearest the edge closest to the light source.

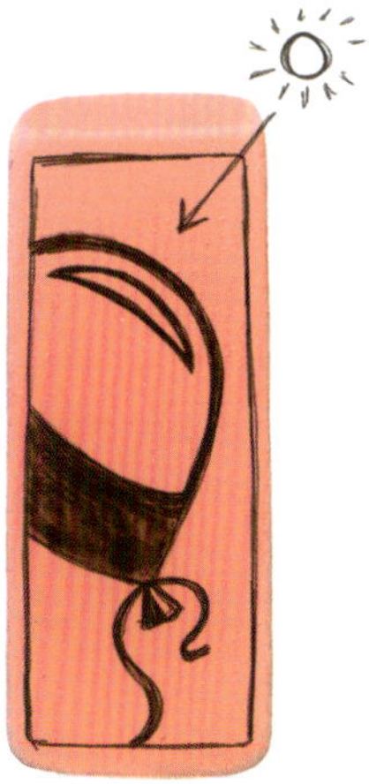

3. Close off your emphasized highlight with a second line.

4. Ink the eraser.

5. Stamp!

When Light Sources Don't Matter

In every section of this book, I have been telling you a rule and immediately telling you to break it. This section on lighting is no different. Reminder: The art you are making belongs to you. It is yours to experiment with and explore, and nobody's rules get to tell you what to do. I have only offered them as steppingstones to cross the river that separates you from fearless creativity. Once you get across that river, the rest is up to you.

When don't light sources matter? Choosing a dramatic light source is a stylistic choice. It is mostly used when creating an environmental-style artwork. If you are carving a floating object or a line drawing, you aren't going to need to think about light sources at all, because the artwork you are creating is all about the lines. You won't need to worry about a light source if you are carving utilitarian stamps, like a star-rating bar or a to-do list stamp. Stamps that are designs made to embellish your junk journal or to use in multimedia art might also not need a light source.

16

Drawing and Perspective

Understanding perspective in drawing is a classic Art 101 skill; one of the first things taught in every art class. It's also my least favorite lesson, because I don't like the persnickety feeling of a bunch of straight lines. That's my ADHD talking though, because understanding perspective is so important and is honestly something I use every single day as an artist—even in the doodles I make on envelopes while I am on hold with the bank. (Just kidding, I don't call people on the phone. But my point stands.) Perspective is artistic bread and butter that we all need to study and understand so we can level up our art and make really cool things.

My main issue with drawing perspective lessons is all of the straight lines—they are just emotionally difficult for me. (You think I am being facetious right now, and maybe I am a little bit, but enough about me.) Here's what is really cool about eraser art: the drawing space is so incredibly tiny you cannot actually use a ruler to measure any lines. A ruler is just too big! But we don't need to use a ruler, because we are working with such a small space that it is so beautifully easy to draw generally straight lines freehand. And we will be carving over those lines anyway, so nothing actually needs to be perfect.

If you haven't learned about drawing perspectives before, you now know it has something to do with lines. So, my emotional baggage aside, let's talk about it.

Using perspective tricks and vanishing points is the key to creating the feeling of a whole world in a tiny piece of artwork. I mentioned earlier that I love creating tiny pieces of artwork that feel like you are looking through a window, seeing only a small piece of something that is actually much larger. Using perspective is one way to do that.

Drawing Landscapes with Perspective

Landscapes are a classic start to understanding perspective, because if you have ever been on a road trip, you have already spent time within the lines you are about to create, and that helps a lot when you are learning a new concept. Think about your last road trip, or just the last time you were on a straight road looking into the distance. Picture in your mind the horizon line. Now, think about the lines on the road. There are lines along both sides of the road, and lines up the center of the road. Now, think about what the lines do as you look toward the horizon line. They get closer together the farther away from you they are. If you have ever been in the Southwest, you've seen the flat desert landscapes and the highways that traverse it in such straight lines they seem to go on to infinity; it can be difficult not to have an existential crisis as you speed along. On these flatland highways, we can see until the road vanishes into the horizon. In art, when learning about how to create perspective in your drawings, the key to mastering this technique is called the vanishing point. It is that point ahead of you as you drive endlessly through the desert that you can never reach. The point where the road, and everything you can see seems to be leading to, until it disappears once again into the distance.

Drawing a Landscape

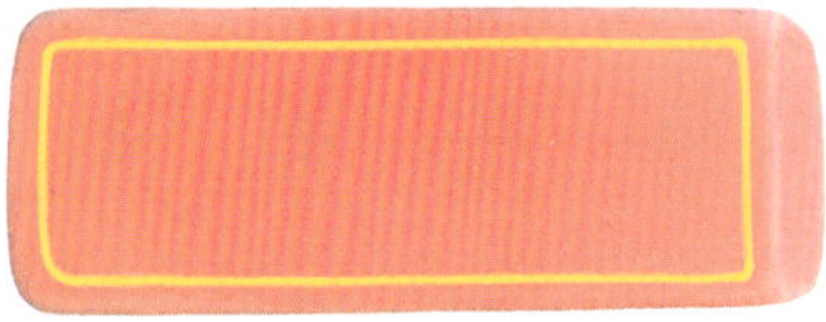

1. Create your border, if you want one.

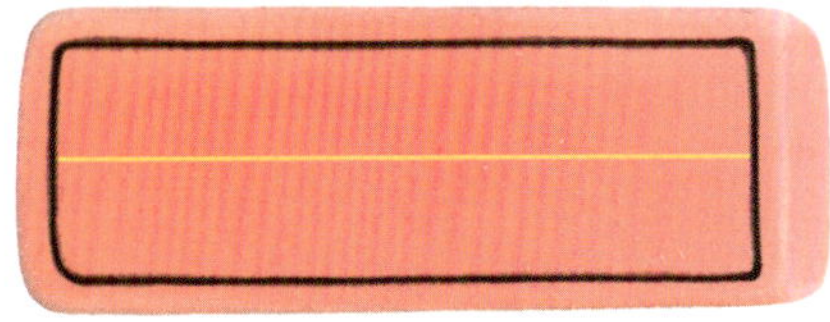

2. Draw a horizontal line across the center of your eraser. You officially have a landscape. Everything above that line is sky. Everything below that line is the earth. That line is called your horizon line, where earth and sky touch.

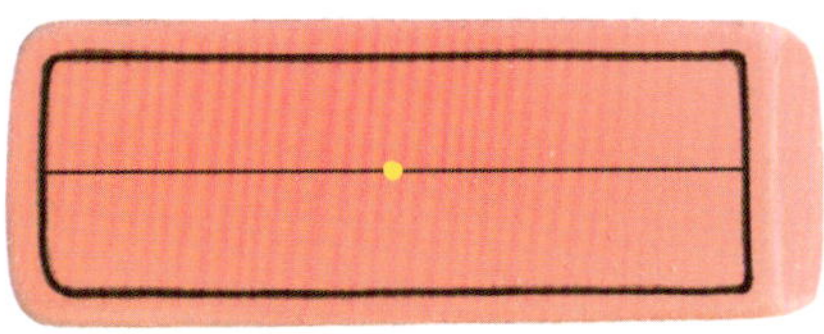

3. Draw a dot in the exact center of that line.

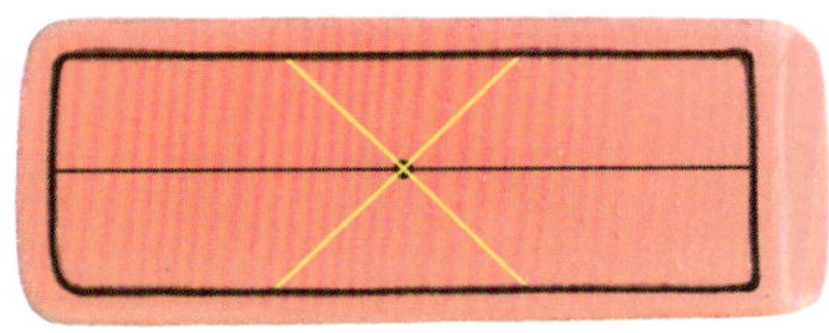

4. Draw an X over that dot and extend those lines all the way to the edge of the eraser. You just drew your road.

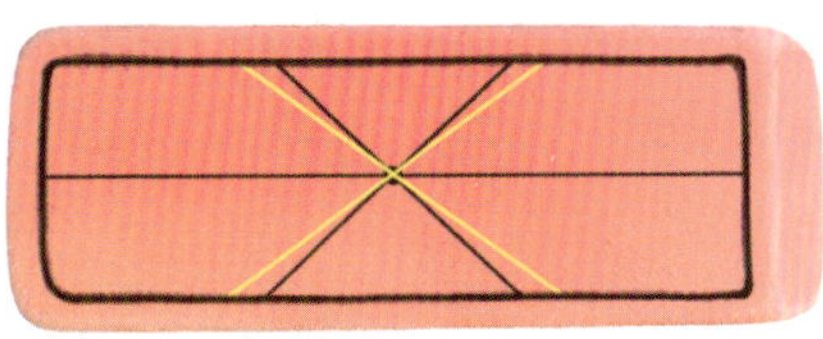

5. Draw a second X over the dot, slightly wider than the first. Now your road has edge lines.

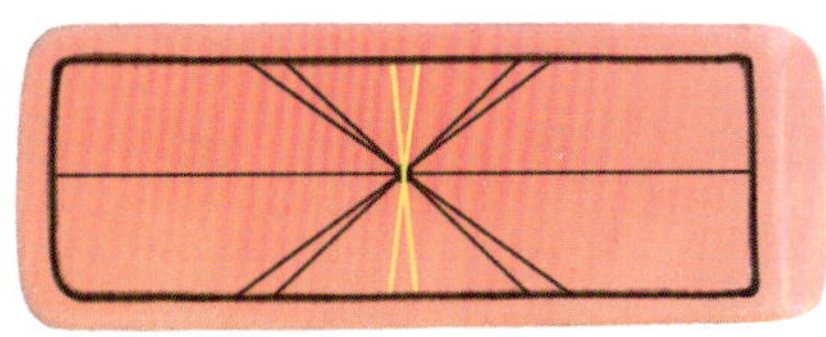

6. Draw a third X over the dot, as tall and skinny as you can. Now your road has center lines.

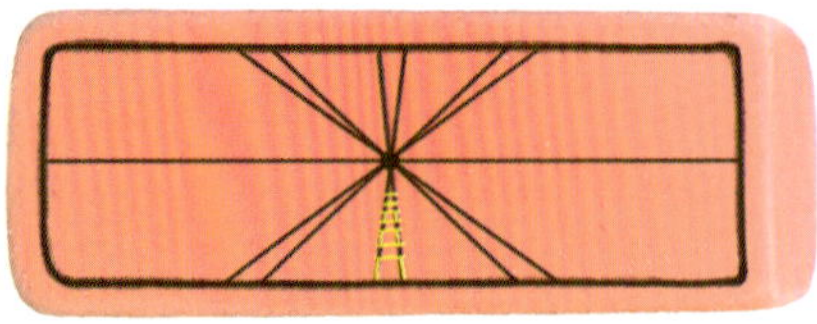

7. Draw small horizontal lines across your center line, farther apart at the bottom of your eraser and getting closer together the closer they get to the dot.

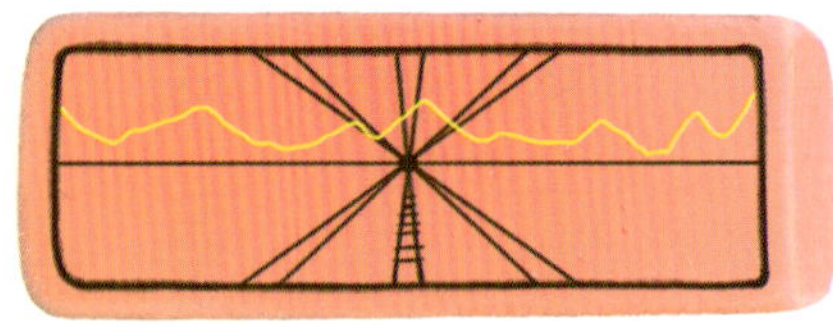

8. Draw a squiggly line near and above the horizon line. You just made mountains!

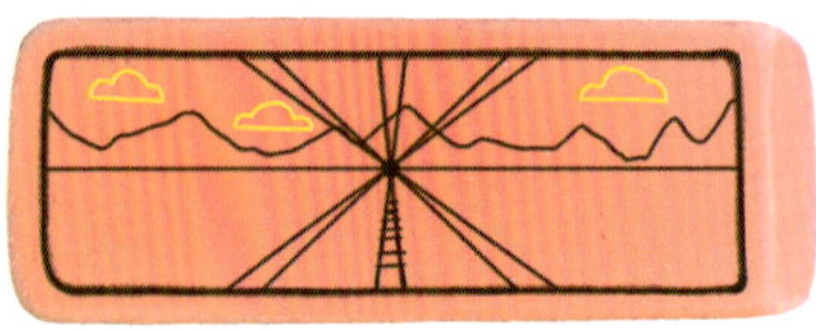

9. Draw three little cloud shapes in the sky. That looks nice.

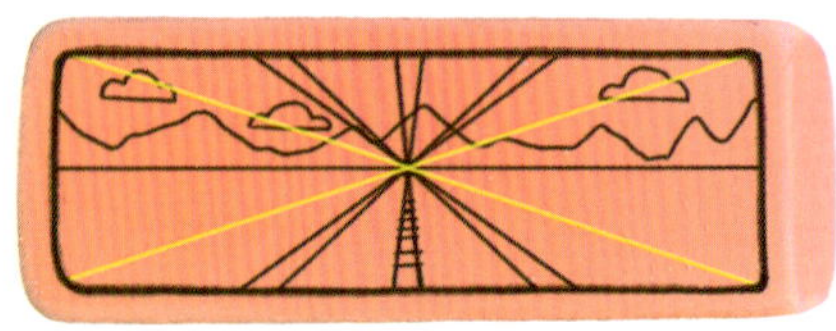

10. Your barren highway landscape might benefit from some foliage, but you want to make sure that your little shrubs also work correctly with the illusion of perspective you are creating. Draw another X over the dot, this time so wide that it reaches both corners of your eraser.

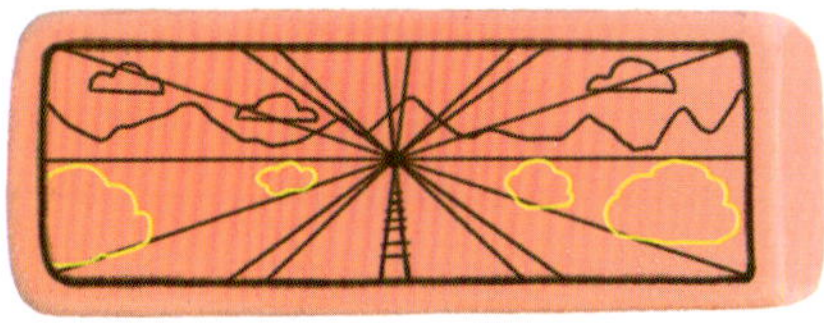

11. Draw some little shrub shapes, keeping them between the corner lines and the horizon line, and between the corner line and the road edge lines. The shrubs closer to the border will be larger and will get smaller closer to the center at the same rate as the road is shrinking. You now have a full landscape and can begin carving.

12. Let's take a look at the final layout without our guidelines. You don't need to try and erase the guidelines before carving, you can just carve over them. But for the sake of mastering this concept, let's take those guidelines away so we can see clearly what we just created!

13. Now we can color in the sections we want to be positive space, so we can decide what we are carving away and what we are leaving behind.

14. Carve it out!

15. Stamp it!

Now that you have created this superneat and iconic road trip landscape, you can use this set of steps to create any kind of landscape or cityscape that you want! Here's the short version for you reference later:

1. Horizontal line (horizon line) across the center of your eraser.
2. Dot (vanishing point) right in the middle of that line.
3. A series of Xs at different widths.
4. Use those X lines as guides for the size and angle of your chosen details.

Example 1: Sonoran Hiking Trail

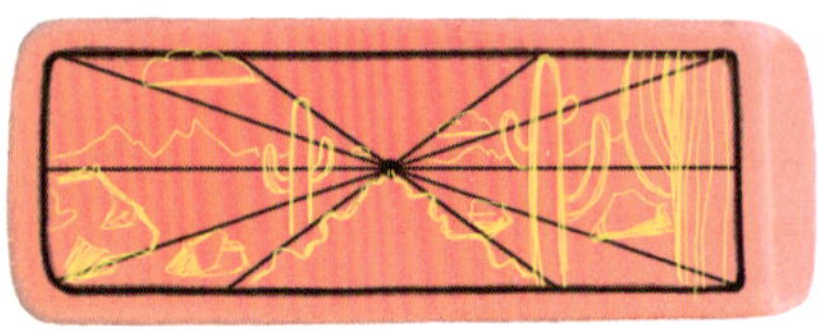

Example 2: Greenhouse

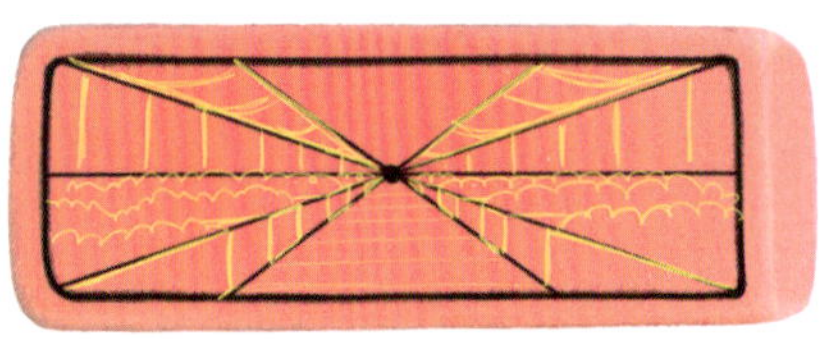

Using Vanishing Points to Create Depth

We know how to make an epic landscape by putting our vanishing point in the middle of the eraser, but here's a secret (it's not a secret, really): there are no rules about where that vanishing point goes! You don't even have to put the vanishing point on the eraser itself. You can place it outside of the border and it will still serve as a guide to flawlessly create depth. Say what? Yes, it's true and best utilized on a sketch paper before drawing directly on your eraser. Go grab your sketch paper, I'll be here waiting patiently.

1. Trace your eraser onto a sketch paper.

2. Draw your border if you are planning to use one.

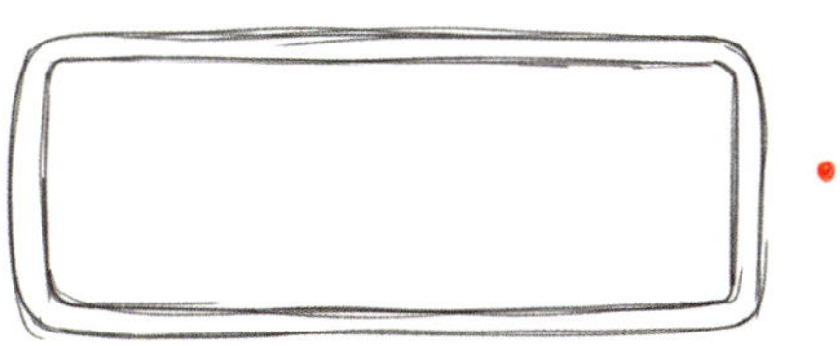

3. Draw a dot to the right of your eraser outline (or literally anywhere, don't be afraid to experiment).

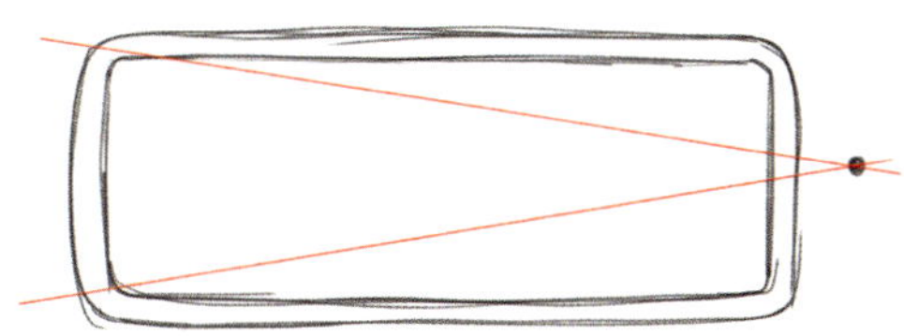

4. Draw three Xs over the dot with varying widths, making them long enough to also cross over your eraser outline.

5. Draw your chosen subjects within the guidelines you created.

6. Transfer or redraw your sketch onto your eraser surface.

7. Carve fearlessly.

8. Print.

Now you can create the illusion of depth in your carvings with literally anything you can dream of. You can use this to draw a row of saguaros, a crate of strawberries, or umbrellas on a beach. But wait, we aren't done.

Using Two Vanishing Points to Give Perspective

Now that we know how to use a vanishing point outside of the eraser, I am about to hand you even more power. Are you ready? Because you can use more than one vanishing point in your sketches to make really neat things happen to your art! I know I said a lot of mean things about learning how to use perspective in drawing at the beginning of this chapter, but the fact is that I love using this technique so much, sometimes I make art just to do it. I want to use this two-vanishing-point technique on as many things as I can think of. It is a cheat sheet. It is magic. It makes me feel like a more-skilled artist than I think I am.

1. Trace your eraser outline onto your sketch paper.

2. Make a border, if you want one.

3. Pick two random places to place dots.

Tip

If you want to create the effect of looking down on something, like a book on a desk, place your dots above the center of the eraser. If you want to create the effect of looking up at something, like a building or a super-sweet taco truck, place your dots below the center of the eraser.

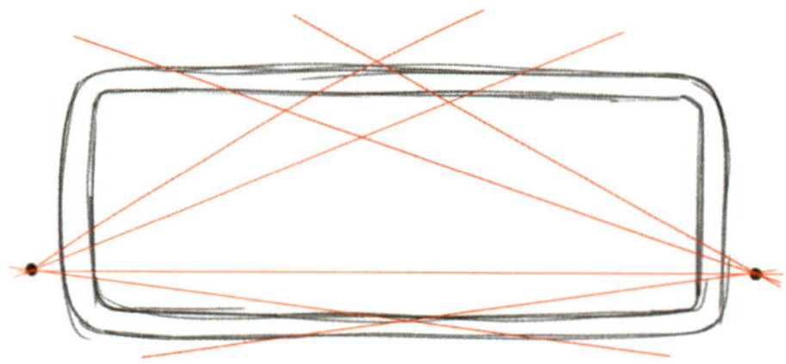

4. Draw three Xs over the center of your individual dots so that they will cross over the eraser sketch, allowing these lines to cross over each other if that's how they land. You can also draw a line between your two dots to create a horizon line.

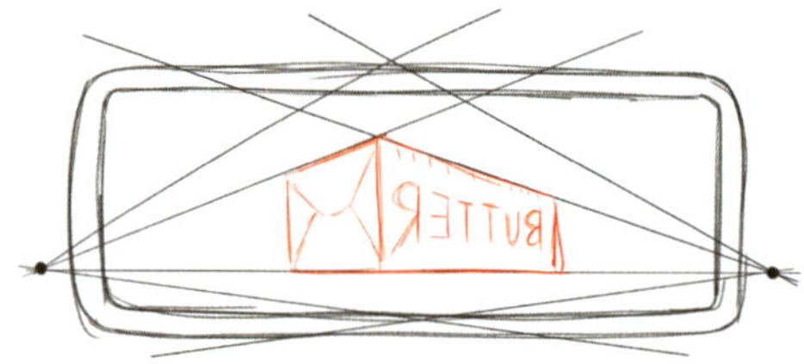

5. Making the widest area between all of these intersecting lines the corner of your subject, sketch your subject, using the guidelines as the lines for your object.

6. Transfer, carve, and print your image.

Using Size to Create Depth

I know this knowledge to creating the illusion of depth with vanishing points and perspective lines has made us feel incredibly powerful. Before all of this power goes to our heads, let's recognize that sometimes we want to create a dramatic, impactful illustration but just can't emotionally handle the geometry of it all. That is absolutely fine, because the truth is, mostly when I am making time to be creative, I am basically in an emotional crisis and am using art as therapy. Sometimes we just need to draw some little flowers and not think about it all. So, after I have taught you all of these magnificent things, you can create the same effect on a whim, without a plan, and you can do that by simply making your objects different sizes.

The rules for this are simple, and you can break these rules too, because it is your art to do with what you will. In general, when doing a little doodle, whatever you want to be in the foreground can be larger. Anything in the background or father away can be smaller and be partly behind the bigger thing in the foreground. You can follow a general line, similar to what we did with the perspective guidelines, or you can place your subjects randomly.

For this example, let's look at a field of flowers from two different angles. In figure A, we are looking out across a field.

The largest flowers in the foreground are at the bottom, and as they get closer to the horizon line they will be smaller. Don't panic, just doodle. Because these are the doodle rules. Smaller at the top, bigger at the bottom. In figure B, we are looking down on that field of flowers from where we are standing.

As we look down, some flowers are taller, so they are closer to our eyes, and thus slightly larger. Some flowers are shorter, farther away from our eyes and below the taller flowers, so they might be tucked behind the larger ones. They are spaced randomly, because that is how they are growing, and the size doesn't determine the placement. Doodle those flowers with fearless abandon.

A B

17

Multi-Stamp Sets

We have talked extensively about all the ways to create art within the boundaries of the standard eraser shape, but I've been holding out on you. Why? Because the most satisfying thing to do with a pink eraser is actually to CHOP IT INTO A BUNCH OF TINY PIECES! Use that blade in your kit that looks like a tiny axe to chop and hack and slice through the soft rubber to make a collection of even smaller erasers that work in tandem to create a variety of pictures and art. Creating these tiny pieces of a whole is so much fun, because after the joy of carving the elements of the collection, it is an interactive printing process that can change every time you use your stamps. The opportunities of what you can carve and how you can use them are endless.

It can be a fun challenge to puzzle your image elements onto a single eraser and see how much you can fit, like the tiny alphabet stamps. It can also be fun to create larger images using a single eraser for each part of the image, like a sunflower. You will also find that, as you begin creating different shapes, you can use stamps across sets and turn one stamp into endless pieces of art. Take this flower stem for example:

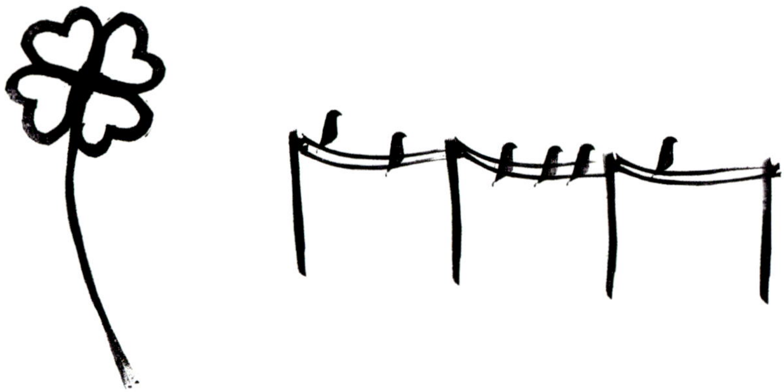

It started as part of a flower and then became a power line. It could also become a string of lights or a smile on a silly face. The possibilities are as endless as your imagination, and puzzling together stamps like a mosaic on your print is bound to get you thinking creatively.

To understand how to organize a set of stamp designs on a minimal number of erasers, let's take a look at the construction of the ice cream cone stamp set. I used two erasers to create this set. I carved the largest two elements, the cone and the ice cream scoop, onto one eraser.

On the second eraser, I carved the smaller pieces, the toppings: a dollop of whipped cream, a cherry, and some sprinkles.

NOTE

It is important to carve the design out of the eraser before cutting the eraser apart, so that you can handle the eraser effectively. Once the smaller pieces are cut, it can be near impossible to carve them safely. When cutting the erasers apart, you may want to use your knife blade to shave down the excess eraser so that you can see clearly as you stamp your designs together to create an image.

Ice Cream Cone Stamp Set

The ice cream cone stamp set came into being simply so I could make the tallest ice cream cone stack I have ever seen, and as I continued to stamp another and another and another scoop of ice cream on my paper, my kids laughed out loud, as if I was attempting to stack them up in real life.

It was worth every moment of the carve to entertain them. This is a fun stamp for embellishing notes or adding to multimedia art because you can use many different color inks on the various elements of the set, or you can color in your stamps after the ink is dry!

Flower Stamps Set

Flowers are a fun subject when breaking down shapes into black and white stamps because they come in such a wide variety of shapes and sizes. Flowers have three main elements, not including the stem.

The petals, leaves, and center allow for endless carving and mixing and matching. Take some time to notice wildflowers on your next walk or visit a local plant nursery when you need to get out of the house. Take notice of the shapes and textures of different flower species. See the color patterns and where petals may have white and color intermingled in different shapes. You could make your positive space in your carvings where the color on the petals is and carve out any white areas. You could ignore color altogether and carve the texture of the petals. Do the petals have wrinkles? Do they have ridges or are they smooth? Bring a sketchbook with you and draw outlines of the petal shapes, the patterns in the flower center, and the different shapes of leaves.

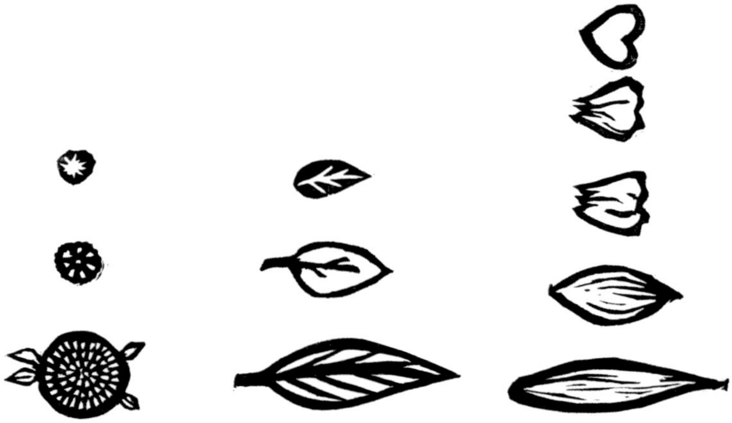

If you haven't already noticed, you will be amazed at how many different shapes of leaves there are. I am a slow hiker because there are just so many shapes of leaves to look at! If you are out and about without a sketchbook, snap a couple of pictures of interesting flowers on your phone to reference later.

Alphabet Stamp Set

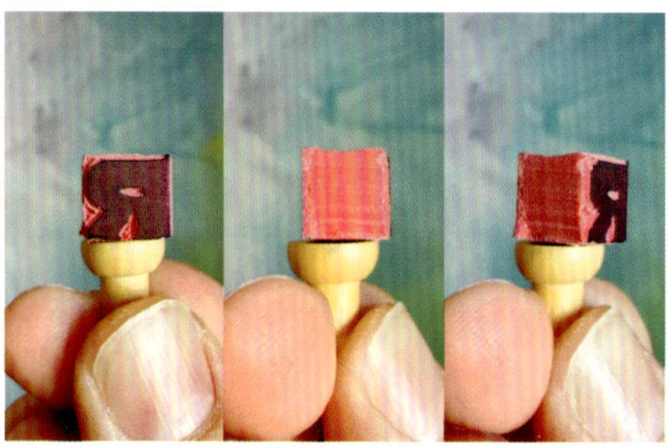

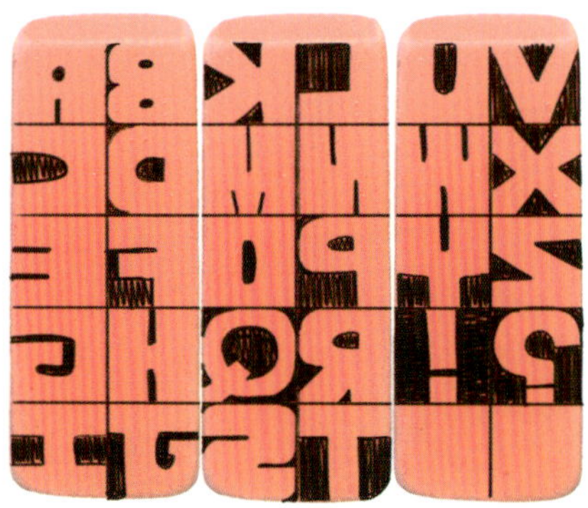

This set of stamps is so fun to carve, and a bit difficult to use, because they are so small. If you love them, and want to use them often, you can stick a thumbtack into the side of the stamps to give them a handle.

Though these are tricky to handle, they are satisfying to create, and a stylistic joy once printed. I can't wait to use them in zines! I created these miniature letters by splitting the eraser down the middle longways.

But you could also make the letters much larger by breaking them into thirds, getting three letters out of each eraser instead of the ten letters per eraser that I managed here.

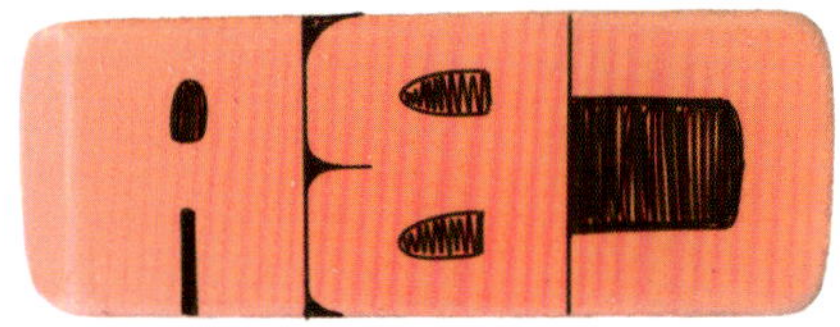

Word Stamp Sets

If you are a fan of creating your own stationery or zines, or using words and phrases in your junk journal or multimedia art, you can carve whole words into individual stamps as well. Think about words you use often (and, the, to) and start with those, and then you can go on to create words for any messages you'd like to.

Tip

Write the word on all sides of the eraser, and sort them in alphabetical order.

Maze Stamp Set

Creating mazes can feel incredibly intimidating, but it is really fun to do because it entails just carving straight lines. All you have to do is make sure you have at least two exits from each eraser (if you want to be more complex and create more, go for it!). When designing your eraser maze blocks, you can line them up against each other to make sure the exits match. If you want to make a variety of maze block stamps for creating a more complex puzzle, you can shift the erasers you are sketching around to connect in new ways as you add more blocks to the collection. You can make the maze as long as you want, and, when printing, you can repeat blocks wherever you want, just be sure to match up the exits.

Comic Strip Builder Set

Creating an itty-bitty comic strip on napkin notes to your loved ones is so much fun! These blocks are also one of the easiest to carve because you are just creating border shapes. Here are four border examples, including a speech bubble, but you can create whatever shapes you want. Stamp these shapes into a stack on a napkin, sticky note, or scrap paper, and leave a little cartoon doodle for your kids, friends, or coworkers to find!

Funny Face Stamp Set

Googly eyes; angry eyes, wacky, wibbly wobbly eyes; noses; mouths; and ears are all things you can carve in endless shapes and designs for a funny faces stamp set. You can stamp the faces onto doodles, onto images pulled from old magazines, or in notes to your friends. Carve the eyes together onto a single stamp or make a variety of single-standing eyes for mixing and matching. Oh, and don't forget to carve some rosy cheeks, sprigs of baby hair, or a little bow to enhance your silly faces.

Speech Bubble Chat Stamp Set

With just two stamps in this set you can invite your date to prom, check in with your friends, or make funny animations. These little speech bubbles are perfect for zines, snail mail, cartoons, or comics. You can even use them with other stamp sets, giving your flowers or funny faces the ability to speak!

18

All-In-One Stamps

Unlike a manufactured stamp that is glued to a block of wood, when we carve stamps from erasers, we have access to every side of the eraser to use to our whim. Soon after carving my first stamp, I had an immediate urge to make a stamp that I could essentially roll across a page and make a larger image with. I never did this, because I didn't want to make something that was bound to be incredibly messy; the purpose of that manufactured block is to get an evenly stamped image, but also to keep our fingers out of the ink. I did, however, design a multi-sided stamp that I could use without too much mess: I only used three of the six sides, so I could hold onto the eraser without unintentionally spreading ink across my entire workspace. That said, if you have the urge to try out something inevitably messy, don't let me stop you! If you also have the urge to use every centimeter of the eraser surface for art, absolutely, unequivocally do it.

I am going to teach you how to make a two- or three-sided stamp in which all of the carvings work together for a single purpose. It is an idea that just feels right, but also, I am a messy person, and it is just better for me if things that belong together are literally attached. Therefore, I created stationery stamps that serve a specific purpose and have interactive sides! These two interactive stamp ideas are so fun to use with different color inks if you have them!

Before we begin, carve the small sides of the eraser first and do a test stamp to determine if you need to cut away from the eraser's main surface before you sketch your design. This unwanted edge can print accidentally when carving adjoining sides of the eraser because that corner angle is shared between the two sides. We simply need to carve that corner away, and that is most easily done by carving the small sides first.

To-Do List Stamp

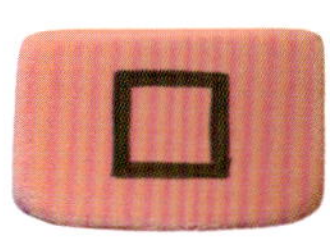

1. Sketch a square with an open center on one end of your eraser.
2. Sketch a check mark on the other end of your eraser.

3. Carve out both ends all the way to the edges, including the corner shared with the main eraser surface.

4. Sketch the "To-Do" on the main side of the stamp, using the tips from Chapter 9 if needed. Make sure to draw all of your words backward.

5. Carve out the "To-Do."

Star Rating Bar Stamp

1. Sketch a single star on the end of your eraser.

2. Carve out the star, keeping the center of the star as positive space. Be sure to cut all the way to the edges, including the corner shared with the main eraser surface.

3. Sketch the star bar on the main surface of the eraser.

4. Carve out the star bar by (a) first outlining the border, (b) then outlining the stars, (c) then removing the center of the stars, and, finally, (d) carving out the negative space around the stars. The stars must be hollowed out so they can be filled in later in your journal as you rate things.
5. If you want, you can also carve a half-star on the other eraser end for a wider variety of rating options.

19

Triptych Prints

Erasers are small, but that doesn't mean your art has to stay tiny! We already learned how to carve sets of stamps to use as building blocks to make larger images, but you can also create a bigger image in a different way—by building a triptych of erasers! A triptych is an arrangement of three separate artworks that are displayed together. These images can be separated by individual borders, with different but related artwork that creates a scene when they are placed side by side. Or they can also be a borderless arrangement that can be stamped side-by-side or even glued together before carving. This method is an innovative way to enlarge your carving surface while still working with erasers, or a fun way to connect your artworks during an art challenge. Classic triptychs consist of three panels, which is what we will be exploring in this chapter, but the connectivity between your eraser artwork can be in whatever size, shape, or arrangement you want.

The key to creating effective triptychs is to plan how and where the panels will connect. Will there be details that flow from one eraser to another? Will they be different subject matter, but in the same style and layout? Will they simply be different elements of a single scene? Will you separate them with individual borders or, perhaps, one large border that spans across all three erasers? Planning out these details is what will take your erasers from simply being similar artworks next to each other to a single artwork that pushes your creative boundaries and gets you thinking outside the oddly elongated, little pink box.

Connecting Scenes Across Surfaces

If you are planning to enlarge your surface area for a single image, you can tack your erasers together side-by-side with glue or just hold them together carefully as you sketch your design. You will want to ensure that the details that cross from one eraser to another are carved carefully for a flawless print.

If you are creating a connected scene, but will be using individual borders, you can draw your design first, and then draw your borders over your sketch as the final step before you begin carving.

If you want to create one large border that crosses over all of your erasers, line up your erasers when you sketch the connecting border lines as well.

Connecting Scenes without Connecting Details

You can absolutely build a set of erasers that can be printed together without passing details across borders. By keeping the carving style similar, and sizing your subjects out to match, it is possible to create a scene one eraser at a time that, when printed side-by-side, will create a larger image. It can be fun to build elements that go together, like making each eraser an individual rowhouse, or creating different items you might see in a dinner spread or on a charcuterie board. This is a great way to challenge yourself if you dive into a 30-day community art challenge, by figuring out how to connect different daily prompts within one scene.

Telling a Story

A triptych is a great way to tell a story by adding a different moment to each eraser. It is also a fun way to embellish a list, because we all know that writing out a loved one's favored recipe is just the same as telling their story. Imagine carving out an eraser for each ingredient and stamping your finished artwork into a cookbook, or printing a favorite family recipe out, decorated with your own carved art prints.

What an incredible gift that would be to share. This can also be taken further, for example, by using erasers to create an acrostic poem, carving an eraser for every letter in a name or one for every letter of the alphabet.

Gathered Portraits

Creating a triptych of carvings separated by individual borders is also a fun way to create portrait-style artwork. This could be made with your favorite book characters or your favorite drinks on a menu. Simply frame each subject just like the others, create that matching border on each one, and you have a collection of portraits literally made for each other.

Tip

Simple glue, such as a purple glue stick, is enough to tack erasers together while sketching and carving your connected triptych.

If you print your glued triptych erasers while still connected, the curved edges will cause a gap between each eraser. To print the triptych completely flush, you will want to pull your erasers apart after carving and line them up individually as you print. Whether to keep the erasers glued together or not is a choice based on the shape of your erasers, and each option has its pros and cons. Printing all erasers while attached keeps them perfectly lined up but creates a gap (if your erasers have curved corners) and allows for more shifting and accidents during printing. Separating your erasers before printing can make lining up the prints more difficult, but allows for more accurate quality of printing, as well as allowing the images to be flush against each other.

Printed while glued together

Pulled apart and Printed individually

20

Oddly Sized Eraser Art

I don't know about you, but I love it when things are not the size they are supposed to be. Throughout my artistic career, my joy has been making a thing and then making it as big as possible and as small as possible. We all love a tiny thing, and an oversized thing. Massive spell-book-style journals? Yes. Tiny tea sets? My most prized childhood possession. Humanity loves oddly sized things. I recently saw a tiny metal book that folded open to become a gold bracelet made by Victorian-era jewelers. Also, look at historic art and architecture: the pyramids? The Nazca Lines? We all love an outrageously large or small

piece of art, and we have for centuries. Taking on this challenge ourselves is good for us. We are already pushing ourselves by carving into these tiny, oblong erasers, so shifting out of that mindset into something larger or even smaller is a great exercise to get our creative juices flowing in different directions.

My husband calls this "Stumping your brain." What does that mean? We have no idea, and we laugh about that. But it became a mantra he spoke regularly to himself to help him break out of his autopilot habits in order to become more present. He started taking different routes to work, he started shouting, "Stump your brain, Serena!" when I did not want to go for a walk after dark in the cold. It has also been spoken softly, when he took my hands and pulled me out into the sun to help me break out of a bipolar depressive state or a panic attack. It isn't a repetitive mantra we need anymore, but it still gets shouted enthusiastically between us when we, two introverts, feel a need to shake things up and become more aware in the present moment. It can be amazing. So, in this section I am going to challenge you to think smaller or outrageously larger. Stump your brain.

Ultramini Stamps: Carving the Eraser Ends

Within the first two weeks of experimenting with carving erasers I tried to carve the name of my friend's botanical shop into the smallest side of the eraser, just to see if I could. I did. I was honestly amazed. So, I tried again and carved the tiniest thing I could think of: a tardigrade (a micro-animal often referred to as a water bear). And even though it wasn't actually microscopic, it was delightfully adorable and brought me a lot of joy. My favorite book binder in my city then offered me a leather-bound sketchbook the size of my thumb-pad so I would have an appropriate place to store my new, minuscule masterpieces.

It is one of my most prized possessions. It is so cute and a joy to carve as small as possible to grace its pages. After I carved the smallest image I could, the tardigrade, I carved the largest—a landscape. But tiny. Taking things out of the expected context and doing something absurd is so fun and such a great way to push our creativity.

Oversized Eraser Stamps

One day I was walking through a craft store and spotted one of those hilariously massive erasers that read "Ooops!" across it. When I picked it up it was heavier than I expected, and I thought about carving it and I laughed out loud. I went home that day with my newly acquired piece of rubber, which oddly seemed much heavier than the rubber slabs designed for carving. When I walked into my studio, I took it out of the bag and just let it drop onto my desk. The *thunk* was as satisfying and loud and clunky as I expected, and I laughed out loud a second time. As excited as I was to carve it into artwork, I found myself intimidated by its size. I wasn't scared of having to carve more area, I was scared I wouldn't use the larger surface to its full potential. Instead of simply drawing something larger than usual, I started to think about carving at the same minuscule size as I do with the regular-sized erasers, but to just add more to my design. So, I created an image that was essentially a nine-in-one. My design could have been nine different tiny eraser carvings, but I arranged all of the subjects together in one big family picture.

Of course, we can carve whatever we want, and not everyone has to be obsessive about challenging themselves to feel validated in carving something larger than a standard eraser. That is a me problem, probably. You can just carve larger if that is what brings you joy. But I found myself wondering if rather than carving a maximum of two or three words into an eraser, I could fit a whole paragraph. Or a speech. Or a poem. I immediately started thinking not just bigger, but more complex. This is where shifting out of our usual mode becomes so fun! Even as I am writing this now my mind is racing with ideas as I think outside of the teeny-tiny pink box.

21

Using Photographs in Printmaking

I love how accessible photography and photography tools have become in recent years, because I get to teach you something really cool. You don't need access to high-end editing programs or expensive apps to learn how to use photographs as a guide in your printmaking, all you need is a phone or a tablet. This trick is incredibly helpful while you are learning to see your subjects in two values—in black and white and in highlights and shadows—in order to translate your image into something you can carve. You can use this technique for line-drawing-style carvings, but it will serve you the most with high-contrast images.

How to Take a High-Contrast Photograph

Remember our chapter on dramatic lighting vs. ambient lighting? Using the ambient-lighting technique on photographs will give you a line-drawing-style image. But using dramatic lighting with deep shadows will give you incredibly fun shapes to carve and explore. You do not need a professional-quality photograph to use this method, because by the end of this process your photograph will look like a punk rock zine. But understanding how to light a quick snapshot of something is going to be fun and will give you a whole new world of ideas with which to work.

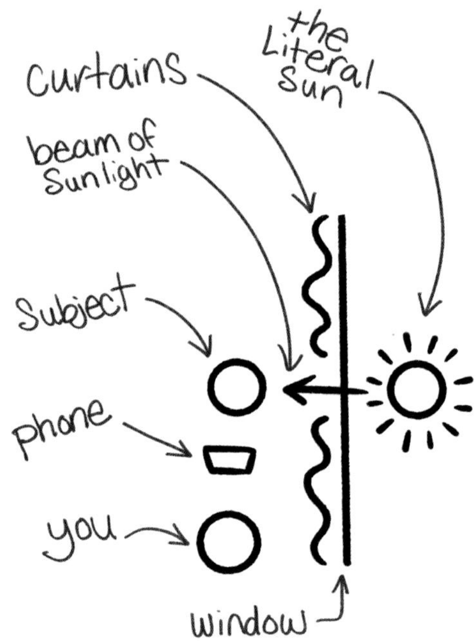

You can take a dramatic, high-contrast photograph of anything, and you can use a window on a sunny day or a desk lamp in a dark room. The trick is to angle the light source to the side of your subject so there is a bright highlight on one side and deep shadows on the other. Sunlight coming in a window will start you off with beautifully crisp lines between your highlights and shadows, but you can also work with softer sunlight coming in your north-facing window as well.

If you are working with softer light and have curtains, close them almost fully, until you have a single beam of sunlight. Place your subject in that beam of light. Angle yourself perpendicular to the window, so the window is to your left or right side and take your photo.

If you have strong sunlight coming directly into your window, place your subject in that light and snap away, still angling yourself perpendicular to the window.

Using a desk lamp or even a flashlight against your subject at night can create the most wonderful high-contrast lighting. Place your desk lamp above or to the side, angled toward your subject, and take your photo 90° from the light source, so you can clearly see the highlights and shadows. If your subject can be turned sideways, do so and angle it below your desk lamp, and then just flip the photo in your app to the correct direction afterward.

Tip

Hold your subject next to your light source and then move it forward and backward. As you move your subject, notice how the amount and angle of the light changes.

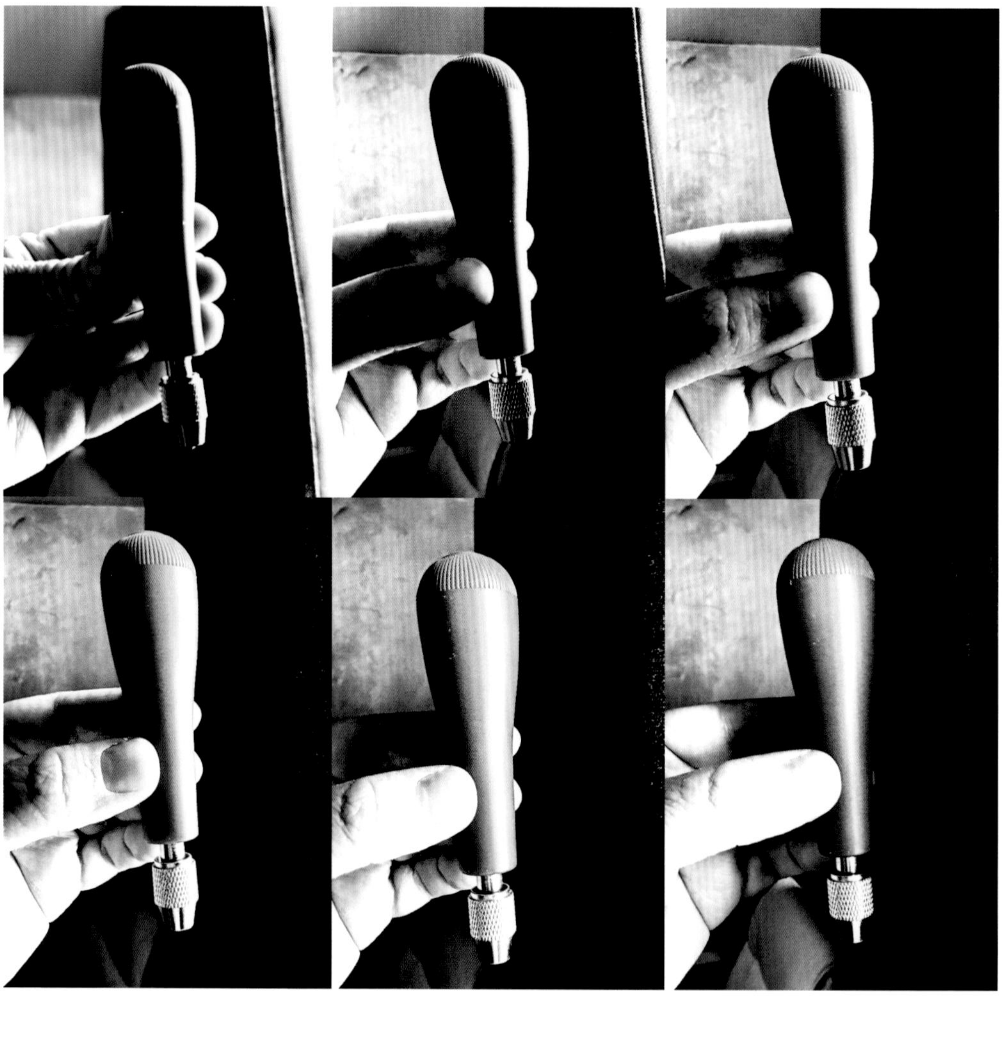

How to Use Your Photograph as a Carving Guide

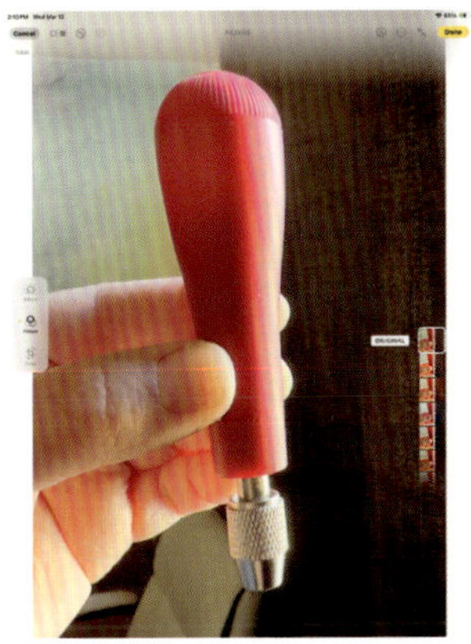

Now that you have your photograph, do a quick edit in your photo app on your phone or tablet.

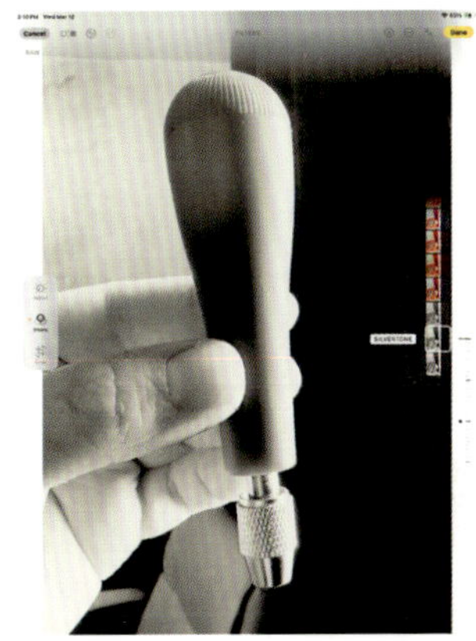

Use a black-and-white filter on the image, choosing the option with the highest contrast. How do you tell if you are choosing the highest contrast filter? It's the one with the darkest blacks and the brightest highlights.

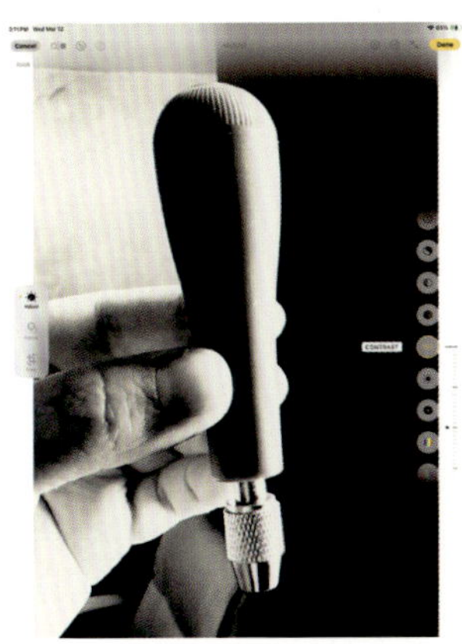

Turn the contrast on your image all the way up, the farthest on the scale it will go. With a good high-contrast image, this will make those highlights and shadows stark, or even to a fully black-and-white image with almost no gray values at all.

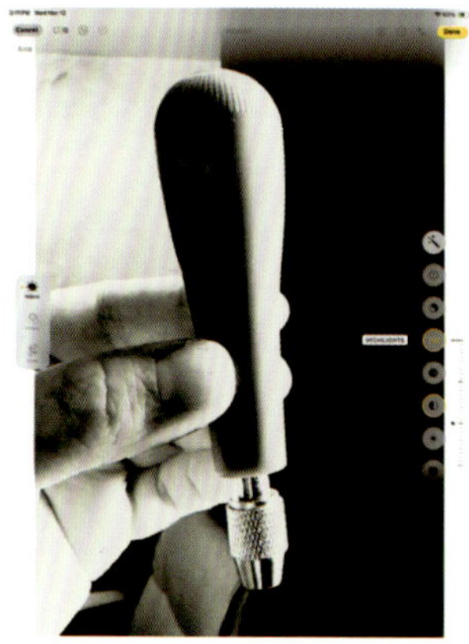

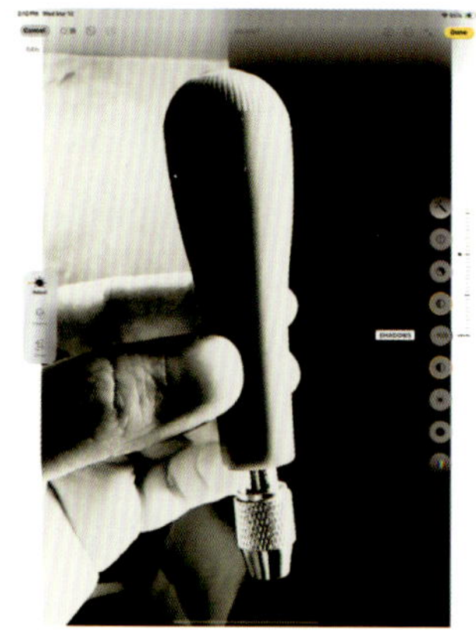

If your image still has a lot of grays, turn your highlights setting all the way up and your shadows all the way down to enhance the contrast.

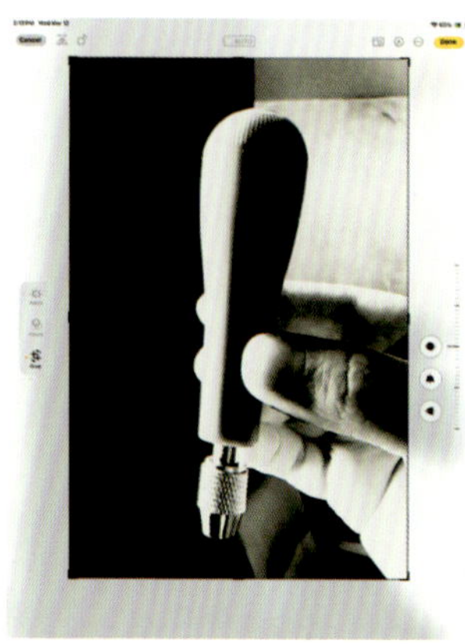

If your image needs to face a certain direction, the last step will be to reverse the image to a mirror of itself.

Now you have an image that is broken down to basic values and you can use the shapes as a guide for your drawing.

22

Reduction Printing

Reduction printing is really cool. It's an intermediate carving concept that gets me excited every time I see it in action, and I couldn't finish this book without introducing it to you. After you make it through all of these lessons, you are going to be on fire with creativity, and I want to lay this offering at your feet so that you can play.

Reduction printing is, by nature, a limited-edition print style. It requires planning and forethought, including ink types and colors (yes, this is not just black ink!), how many prints you plan to create, and how you will break your design down into layers. Why does this require so much planning? Because you will be carving and changing your eraser print throughout the process.

What is reduction printing? It is a process in which you reduce the surface of the eraser while actively printing it out. This process introduces a fun use of color, layers, and details, and combines the techniques and image styles we have talked about in this book in a new way: by printing on top of prints and carving your single eraser as you go. In this process, you will be breaking down an image into multiple layers of color and carving those layers one at a time, beginning with the least detailed and moving to the most detailed. We will be printing between carving each layer. Confused? Don't worry. Let's break it down.

Let's begin with a two-layered image, and then we can move to something more complicated. It should be noted that this printmaking style is usually done with opaque printing inks. You can use those inks, which are applied with a brayer, if you keep your eraser carvings bold in their design. The brayer and ink will fill in any minuscule details scraped across the surface. We will be using basic ink pads, so we will plan our layers with the transparency of color inks in mind. Mixing ink colors is endlessly fun, as their transparency will cause colors to change as you mix them, just like glazing in watercolor painting, but for this first lesson I am keeping it simple.

Two-Layer Reduction Print: Hot Sauce

For the first print, we are going to keep it simple and use only two layers. These could technically be two different erasers in a set that we print together, but I said this was an intermediate technique so let's challenge ourselves and do something scary. Let's go.

Layer One: The background color, with any white highlights cut away.

Layer Two: The detail, in this case, the hot sauce label.

1. Begin by sketching your design onto paper and planning it exactly.
2. Determine which parts of the design will be printed first, and which will be printed second. For the hot sauce packet, we know the red background will be first, and the fine detail of the title on the label will be second.
3. Transfer your sketch onto your eraser surface.

4. Carve out only the minute details that will be negative space—the triangles around the top and bottom edges and the little squiggles, which will create highlights on the wrinkled package.

5. Pause carving and print your design in color ink. Determine how many prints you want to create, because this is your only chance to print this part of your design. Always print a few extra in case of misprints, or if you want to expand the amount of prints you will create.

6 Wipe off any excess ink and carve out all of the spaces around your fine details.

7. Ink your stamp with black ink, line it up over your red backgrounds, and print.

NOTE

I carved away the edges and found it difficult to line up while printing. I believe that leaving a border around the design in this step will make for easier printing, and a more striking final product. (Here is a look at a design with and without a border and how they printed.)

Three-Layer Reduction Print: Daisy

Now, let's raise the reduction print challenge (and fun) with a three-layer print. For this flower, I chose two analogous colors, meaning they are next to each other on the color wheel. Yellow, orange, and black to finish off the design with a bold pop. I have chosen to print the colors lightest to darkest to keep from mixing colors into my ink pads. If you are using opaque printing inks, you can use whatever colors you'd like with each layer.

Layer One: The main daisy color with the background carved away.

Layer Two: Texture on the daisy petals, an outline around the outer edges of the flower and the flower center printed in orange.

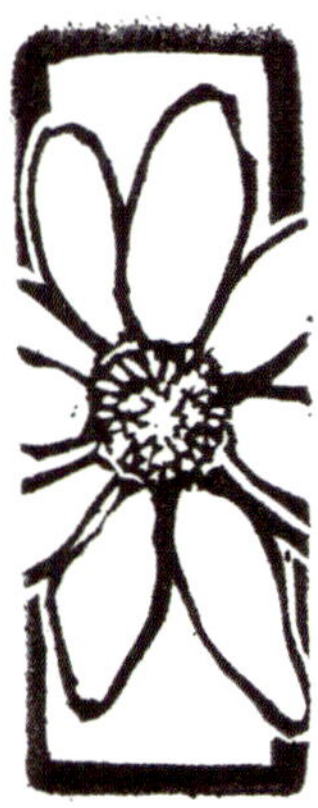

Layer Three: The outline and texture in the flower center.

1. Begin by sketching your design onto paper and finalizing your idea.
2. Determine which parts of your sketch will be in which layer and printed with which color. Above is an example of how I sketched out my plan.

3. Transfer your sketch onto your eraser surface.

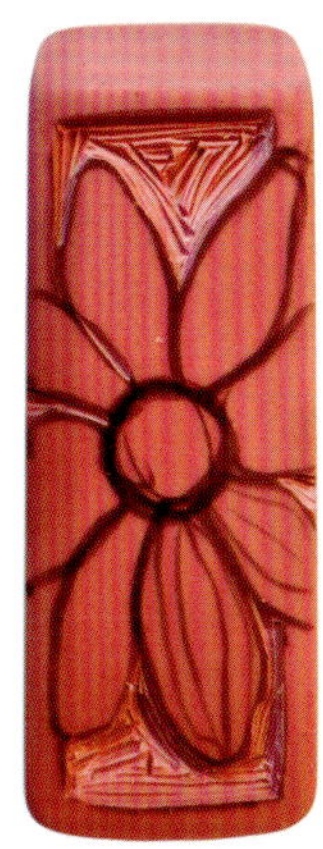

4. Carve out only the blank background around the daisy petals, defining the border shape and the daisy shape.

5. Pause carving. Print your stamp in yellow ink as many times as you want to, and a few more after that in case of misprints.

6. Wipe the ink off your eraser and begin carving out the daisy petals. As you do so, create strips of positive space left behind to give the petal texture. Carve out a small bit of detail in the center of the flower, and a small border around the petals, to separate them from the main border.

7. Ink your stamp with orange ink, line it up on top of your yellow prints, and print it. Make sure you are printing it the right direction. (If you are recording your progress in a sketchbook, you may want to print a single-layer print of just the yellow and orange as well, so you have a reference like this to look back at later.)

8. Wipe the ink off of your eraser. Carve out the entire center of the daisy petals and carve away the border edges as well to make the final outline more delicate. Carve out detail from the entire center of the flower by stabbing and lifting the tiny pieces away.

9. Ink your stamp with black ink, line it up over your prints in the proper direction, and print it. You may want to draw an arrow on the back of your eraser that points upward to ensure you are printing the correct way each time.

NOTE

The border is essentially untouched in this design throughout the entire process and so is printed in every color. This is inconsequential because the final color is black and covers it all. If I wanted to add detail to the border, I would carve away the inside of the border, making it thinner. This would still allow me to use the border to line up a clean print but would print the border in black with an orange edge inside. There is so much we can do as we play with this technique.

Congratulations! You just did something that amazed and intimidated me for a long time. You can explore this in so many ways, play with mixing colors, or print in grayscale with different shades of ink. See how many colors you can fit into one piece of art.

23

Sample Fonts for Text

Sharing thoughts, greeting loved ones with snail mail, signing our artwork, branding a business, creating labels, pressing a maker's mark into clay—all of these can be done with eraser stamps and words. I have taught you how to space out your letters, how to transfer your signature onto an eraser to carve out, and now I offer you these font ideas to get you carving and creating so that you can use your voice and share your message with eraser carving.

Block Lettering

Block lettering is created with the method I taught you in Chapter 12! These are made by spacing out the letters methodically onto the eraser surface and carving out simple notches to create letters from blocks. You'll see a lot of variety in my examples here. Some of the letters are full blocks with just those simple notches; on others I have carved away the block shapes much more to free the letters from the rigidity of being stuffed into squares. This can be done by carving away the space and gives you freedom to shape the letters in your style.

Hatch Lettering

These letters are created by carving away lines, or hatches, as discussed in Chapter 8. You can play freely with this idea by carving hatch lines in any shape, form, or arrangement and in any thickness. By creating my "Tired" stamp with parallel scratched hatches, I made something akin to noise from an old television screen. I guarantee you there is so much more you can do by playing with this method of carving letters.

Bubble Lettering

Bubbly lettering is so fun to carve if you are enjoying the curve technique that I taught you in Chapter 13. These letters can be created in two ways: using the block lettering layout method and then carving your letters down into curvy, friendly shapes, or by writing out your letters, bubbling them up in your sketch, and then transferring them onto your eraser.

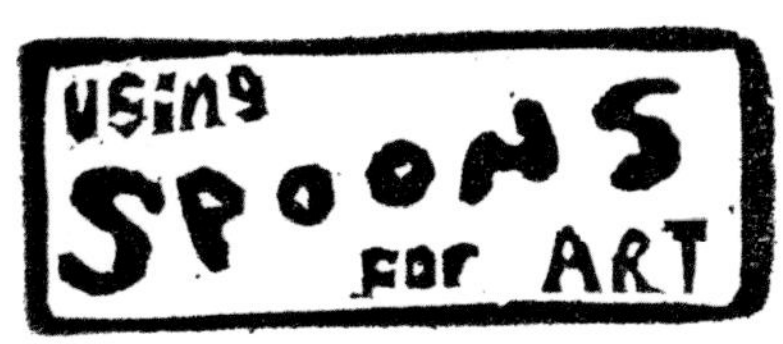

Sketched Lettering

If you want to create a more ambiguous arrangement of words and letters, or make them thinner, you can simply write your letters freehand. When exploring this method, you can map your lettering to create shapes or fun arrangements by drawing guidelines however you want to. You can write your words directly onto your eraser, writing everything backward, or create your arrangement on a sketch and transfer it onto your eraser.

Cursive Transfer Lettering

If you have calligraphy skills, you don't have to learn how to create these while writing backward. Create your calligraphy in ink or digitally and use the transfer methods I taught you in Chapter 6 to transfer them to your eraser for gorgeous signature, decorative letter stamps or wax seal stamps.

Handwritten Transfer Lettering

Your own handwriting is one of the most unique things you can re-create in your stamp carving, and it is as simple as jotting down a note or making a quick signature and then transferring it onto your eraser surface. Remember to thicken your graphite lines on the eraser surface before you begin for ease of carving and a clean final product.

Artistic Lettering

Letters don't always have to be written, sometimes they can be drawn. What is the difference? If you take a minute to look at a single letter and see its unique shapes, angles, and curves, you will realize that every letter is its own picture. And once you realize that, you'll notice that instead of just drawing a letter, you can spend real time drawing it. You can style it. You can turn it into art itself, or you can use letters and words as decoration in part of your artistic composition. In these examples, I used 10K and turned them into those trendy, golden balloons influencers pose with on the Internet. I made the & symbol its own centerpiece, added the word "book" for a little extra detail, and re-created the elvish language in this rendition of the One Ring. Nothing makes you realize how much language is truly art until you try to draw an alphabet you don't know.

24

Creating Your Prints

"What type of ink do you use?" is one of the most common questions I hear because people believe that the clarity and quality of my prints come from the ink. Print quality has more to do with proper printing technique, which we will talk about in a second, but let's talk ink first. Obviously, if you are using a crusty old ink pad you found in the back of your children's craft box, you may not make the greatest prints. Unless crusty and old is what you are going for, which is also amazing. Lean into your vibe, bestie.

Inks

Any printing ink you can find is great, because the best material is the material that will get you creating. If you have it, use it! If you can afford it, buy it. Never feel like a certain type of material is required to create, but you're already a good way through a book about using an innocuous office supply item to make art, so I think we are good here.

Archival ink: I use archival ink, because it has a level of permanence that I have always liked for my projects, and I feel like the black is the most striking I have found. Archival ink is acid-free and lasts the longest without fading. It is washable from surfaces if you spray it with cleaner and wipe it off before it dries.

Printing ink: There are thick, bold inks made specifically for printmaking on a larger scale than what we are creating with erasers. They are so thick you have to use a brayer to spread the ink onto a flat surface, like glass, before you can then use the brayer to apply the ink to the printing block. These inks make beautiful prints and there are versions for paper as well as fabric. I have found that applying these inks with a brayer to my most delicate eraser carvings causes the thicker ink to fill the tiniest details, clogging them up and stopping any chances of a clear print. These inks could work well for bolder carvings without ultrafine details scraped into the surface.

Standard ink: This is the ink your kids probably have in a set of alphabet stamps. It is (hopefully) washable and perfect for teaching your kiddos to carve erasers. These types of inks are great for crafting and junk journaling and are readily available in many colors. These standard inks are probably also the least expensive but may fade in the sun if put on display in a frame. These washable ink pads are what I prefer to put in my carving go-kit in case I accidentally ink something I don't mean to while out and about.

StāzOn: StāzOn ink is popular for crafters and multimedia artists because it is made to print on a variety of surfaces, such as glass, tin, acetate, and other glossy surfaces. This ink is solvent-based and requires a specific cleaner to remove from your erasers after printing. It is versatile and very cool, but I generally avoid it because I don't like to be bothered with deep cleaning if I am carving and printing on the go or for silly little crafts.

ENCREUR À PIGMENT D'ARCHIVAGE
1 pc
StāzOn®
Jet Black
Noir de Jais
Negro Jet
Ranger
ARCHIVAL INK
RE-INKER
JET BLACK
rangerink.com
Ranger
ARCHIVAL INK
ENCRE D'ARCHIVES
• JET BLACK • NOIR DE JAIS •
ACID FREE • SANS ACIDE
PERMANENT INK • L'ENCRE INDÉLÉBILE
WATERPROOF • PREUVE DE L'EAU
Ranger
PIGMENT INK PAD
TAMPON D'ENCRE À PIGMENT
• Glacier White • Blanc Glacier •
BLOCK PRINTING

Ink refills: Whatever ink you choose to work with, do your homework to find out if you can purchase bottles of refill ink. Ranger's Archival sells tiny bottles of refill ink, which I have used on my single stamp pad for two years. It is cost-effective and will save the planet and space in your art supplies drawer.

Paper

I love carving tiny because we don't need anything special or extra to make our prints. We can print on computer paper, random card stock, in planners, a sketchbook, or on torn-out book pages. We can print on fine art papers, seed-bomb paper, or newsprint. If you are looking for the clearest print, you will want a smooth-finish paper. Multimedia and watercolor papers are absorbent and will take ink, but the texture of these papers will show in your print.

Priming the Eraser

Never print your first print on something important! Why? Because the first print is always bad, usually with uneven ink and splotches in the dark areas. When you complete your carving, it will need to be primed before it makes the clearest and most stark print. Priming is not a big deal, just ink and stamp your eraser a couple of times on a scrap paper before printing it onto your fancy paper or craft you are creating. Once your stamp is printing solid black in all of the areas, it is primed and ready to print. When I tested how many times I had to ink and stamp a carving to get the darkest, most clear print, I found that after the fourth stamp the black areas printed flawlessly.

How to Get a Clean Print

Remember all of those cinematic moments where someone at a desk slams a stamp onto the protagonist's application or form and then a bright green "APPROVED" is revealed on the screen? That is not the way to make the best prints.

When I carved my very first linoleum print in my very first art class in college we brought our carvings to class, rolled out the ink onto glass until smooth, and then applied a thick layer of that ink to our linoleum blocks with the brayer. We then lined the paper on top of our block and used the back of a wooden spoon, pressing firmly in little circles across the entire block. The best prints were the ones by people who were the most patient and spent the most time rubbing their paper down onto the block. To get the best prints, we have to bring the same level of pressure, patience, and care into printing our erasers.

Standard stamps purchased at a craft store are mounted on a block, which is easy to hold and creates equal pressure across the stamp. That is not a luxury we have when carving artworks into erasers. Also, we must consider the angled edges on the eraser. Classic pink erasers are not perfectly squared off blocks! They have those funky little angled ends, and we need to remember that when printing and ensure that those funky angles get as much pressure as the rest of the surface. It is also important to note that because we don't have blocks to hold on to, it can be easy to shift the eraser accidentally when printing.

Ink your stamp thoroughly. Carefully place your stamp where you want to print it, anchoring it in place with a finger before letting go.

Press your fingers onto the back of the eraser, giving direct pressure to every part of the stamp. You may need to shift your fingers around the surface top, so remember to keep it anchored so it doesn't get knocked off center.

Press firmly on the angled edge as well.

Lift the eraser straight up so it doesn't smear or ghost ink on the page.

Tip

Draw an arrow on the back of the eraser to make sure you always print it right side up.

Cleaning Your Eraser Stamps After Printing

Stamp maintenance is important but not something that needs to be done immediately, if, like me, you will only ever be stamping with one color of ink. If you like to use your stamps with a variety of ink colors, or with solvent-based inks, cleaning your stamps after printing is essential. I clean my stamps as a batch about every two months, because I only print with one color, and because I am a messy person with ADHD who finds maintenance boring and prefers to skip that step during the actual creative process. Overall, stamp maintenance is up to you, and while I am going to share this knowledge with you, it is not something to stress about.

Why Should You Clean Your Stamps?

If you plan to print with multiple colors of ink, you will want to immediately clean your stamps to keep your ink pads pure and get clean prints in your desired color.

Keeping your stamps clean will avoid ghosting ink onto other stamps in your collection if you keep them stacked together in storage.

Keeping your stamps clean will keep your fingers clean while printing, and avoid accidental fingerprints on your paper during the process

How to Clean Your Stamps

If you are using washable kid's craft ink, you can wash your stamps with soap and water in the sink. Lay out a paper towel and place them face down to dry. If you are using archival ink or solvent-based ink, you can purchase stamp cleaners made to break down these specialty inks. StāzOn and Ranger brands both sell stamp cleaners, which come with a dauber top for gently applying the cleaner to your eraser stamps. There are stamp scrubbers on the market, but these are designed for classic stamp rubber, which is much firmer than our pink erasers, and can scratch the surface of your carvings. I use a microfiber cloth instead.

Dab your cleaner onto the eraser surface and let sit.

Wipe your eraser stamp onto a fluffy, microfiber cloth until clean.

Rinse stamps under cold water.

Set face-down on a paper towel to dry.

Tip

During the stamping process, I set my stamps face down on a paper towel so I don't accidentally ink my tabletop while creating.

ART
PINK ERASER ART
Ya MAMA!
Using SPOONS for ART
MAKE MORE ART
SHOP LOCAL
TUCSON
Artober 2023
Fall
CREEPY
TIRED
Hello, I have ADHD
CALL OUT SEXISM!!
NEVER MORE
RAWR
sonoroks
Desert Sprites
SERENA
Serena

25

Take it Further

The 30-Day Challenge

The thirty-day art challenge trend is where eraser art began, and it continues to be such a fun way to get creativity flowing and build community worldwide. A thirty-day challenge is a great way to get into the habit of creating daily. Even more than prioritizing daily creativity, accessing our creativity each day activates our imaginations in ways only creating daily can.

I have found that taking a class is the best way to get me thinking about art in new ways, partly because of the daily creation, but also because when you take a class you surround yourself with like-minded creators. Over the years, I have participated in and hosted many timed art challenges, and some of my favorite online artist friends have come from these moments. Connecting with other creatives is one of my favorite things about being an artist. I love seeing the way other people can take the same prompt or assignment or material and do something wildly different than me. I love comparing and discussing artworks or assignments, because sharing ideas between members of the creative community expands our imagination and understanding of a craft. It also helps us spark new ideas, which usually leads to trying new things or challenging ourselves further.

Choosing to create daily unlocks a creative flow that can open up to us, and so setting a time challenge for ourselves is a great way to access that. Limiting our challenge to thirty days is important because it feels less intimidating than "I need to create every day." Setting goals and challenges for ourselves requires a set expectation, otherwise we find ourselves looking into a void making it is easier to quit because we can't see a finish line.

Thirty-day challenges are something you can set for yourself, something you can choose to host on social media or with your friends or local community, or something you can easily find online to join. Members of the eraser carving community often volunteer to cohost eraser carving challenges through the community Instagram account I run, @pinkeraserart, which is a great place to begin connecting with like-minded creatives who love carving itty-bitty artworks.

Getting Started on a Pink Eraser Art Challenge!

What better challenge is there than to dive into learning pink eraser art with the guidance of this book? This challenge follows each section of this book and will take you through all of the concepts, one day at a time. You can count the activities and ideas included in each section of the book as your challenge artworks, or you can just use the themes of each section to push your own creative practice.

This list of prompts is for you to dive into a thirty-day art challenge no matter when or where you are! Not on social media? That's fine, you can always challenge yourself without having to share it online. If you are on social media, and you do want to share, post your daily challenge artwork with #PinkEraserClubChallenge and tag @pinkeraserart! Challenges like this are worthy, even if you don't want to share and just want to quietly enjoy the challenge.

1. Pink Eraser Art
2. Tools
3. Inspiration
4. Border
5. Night vs. Day
6. Transfer
7. Depth
8. Rule of Thirds
9. Front and Center
10. Triangles
11. Style
12. Confidence
13. Petals
14. Letters
15. Curves
16. Details
17. Perspective
18. Dramatic
19. Multi-Stamp Set
20. Multi-Sided Stamp
21. Triptych
22. Odd Sizes
23. Photography
24. Reduction Print
25. Font
26. Handwriting
27. Explore
28. Zine
29. Seal
30. Signature

The 100-Eraser Challenge

I was only a couple of weeks into my first thirty-day carving challenge when I knew it wasn't enough. There is another trend on social media to challenge yourself to create something every day for one hundred days, and so I chose that as my final goal for carving miniature. There are rules and parameters around the 100-day challenge, but I adjusted the goal for myself for a couple of reasons. I changed the rules from having to create every single day for one hundred days to choosing to create one hundred pieces of art, allowing myself days in between. I changed the rules because I have ADHD and have learned that I need to honor the directions my attention goes and to care for my mental health. I also have the joy of carpal tunnel syndrome, which can flare up when I work too hard, too many days in a row. And so, I set a larger goal for myself, while also choosing how to balance such a large goal with caring for my mental and physical health. Some people will disagree with me, but I believe we need to care for ourselves first in all things while still setting goals and challenges to push our growth.

Framing and Tiny Art Gallery Display

The discussion between fine art and crafts can become heated, and I believe that creating these tiny pieces of artwork are a bridge between both. Technically, art is created for aesthetic, decoration, sharing ideas, and expressing emotion. Crafts have always been categorized as anything that is made with a functional use or purpose. Large linoleum block prints have always been made for beauty, sharing ideas, and hanging on walls. Stamps, with their block, handles or the ability to be stuck onto an acrylic block, have always been made to be used by someone else's hands. Stamps are made to decorate, to share messages from person to person, and to assist in someone else's artistic expression or creation. But here we are using the skills of artists to make one-of-a-kind tiny pieces of art. Because of their size, our carvings are portable, like stamps, and can be stored in cookie tins and stowed away for later use. These tiny carvings can be created with a purpose, like our planner stamps or star rating bars, or they can be an artistic expression and proof of technical skill.

When I discovered tiny frames, with precut, beveled matte boards cut to tiny sizes, I was so excited because choosing to take tiny carvings from being stamped in a planner or sketchbook to bring printed on archival paper and properly framed, to me, turned a craft into an art form. The act of honoring our tiny carvings with a proper frame takes them from a silly little thing to something at which to marvel. At least for the viewers of our artwork, because we know our efforts are a marvel already.

My favorite thing is when people have purchased small collections of my tiny prints and framed and hung them like itty-bitty galleries in their homes. We all have one of those awkward, skinny little walls in between spaces, and seeing them become home to my artwork, like a small gallery, brings me so much joy.

Participate in Little Free Art Galleries

Little Free Libraries have led to Little Free Plant Exchanges, Little Free Food Pantries, and Little Free Art Galleries. I absolutely love the way someone can create something simple that can build community in an almost anonymous way. If you aren't familiar with these little libraries, they are small shelves, little sheds, and tiny bird-house-type structures that are weatherproofed and set on display in a public area, usually along a sidewalk. They hold items that are free for anyone to take and are open and available for anyone to add to. They make books, art, or goods available to the community and allow neighbors to share with each other in an unassuming way.

The tiny art galleries often have tiny people inside, who stand and observe the art anyone can hang on the tiny walls. Tiny eraser carvings are the perfect addition to these! One tiny art gallery owner printed out an informational sheet inviting their community to try out eraser art, packed in tiny bags with a single eraser and a zine we made with eraser art from around the globe.

Zine Making

Eraser art is a great way to enhance our zines! What is a zine? Zines are usually small magazines that are made and distributed independently by the author or artist. There are many ways to make zines, and their creators are usually pushing boundaries and breaking expectations. Typically, one zine is created and then scanned and reprinted for distribution within communities to share ideas often deemed taboo or unworthy of mainstream media. Zines have a rich history of giving voice to marginalized communities and are now collectors' items kept in libraries and museums. Zines are revolutionary. They are also the perfect size to share our eraser art, which can be made to enhance and decorate zines, which can be made to share galleries of our tiny eraser carvings.

After I completed my one-hundred-eraser carving challenge, I looked up from my desk to see the revolution I had accidentally started—showing people around the world how accessible printmaking could be. My first response was to make a zine. And so, members of the community that I accidentally inspired sent me their favorite carvings and I built our *Pink Eraser Art Zine* with artwork submitted from artists worldwide.

Zines work outside the gatekeeping of the press, and eraser art is an overlooked art medium; most wouldn't even consider it an art medium. To make zines, artists use copy machines, and we use erasers. It makes sense that these two mediums of expression made from readily available, affordable materials that anyone can access would work together flawlessly.

How to Make a Mini Zine

1. Fold your paper in half and unfold it.

2. Fold your paper in half again in the other direction.

3. Fold in half twice more.

4. Unfold your paper. You should have eight sections.

5. Refold it in half.

6. Cut halfway along the fold.

7. Unfold.

8. Fold again, long ways.

9. Holding both sides of your folded paper, bring your hands together in the center, allowing the folds to bend open, into the shape of an X.

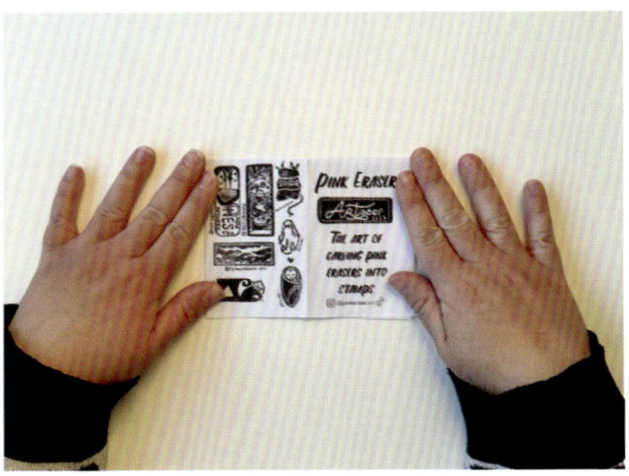

10. Flatten the X onto the table.

11. Fold in half. You now have your tiny zine, with a front, back, and six pages inside.
12. Fill your zine. Print your eraser art, tell a story, share tips and tricks, or write a poem. You can use your zine to express any ideas you would like to share.
13. Unfold your zine. Use a copy machine to create as many copies as you want.
14. Follow steps 1–11 to turn your copies into mini zines.

Junk Journaling

Eraser stamps are so fun for use in journaling if you have made functional stamps for making lists or marking the weekdays or weather, but they are also a really fun addition to multimedia art, collages, and junk journaling. You can make erasers to work with specific themes or just stamp them across a space to add art and texture to a paper you are about to tear in half. You can stamp eraser art like tiles before you paint your main subject, or stamp them in between water-colored layers to add secret messages to your artwork. You can use your stamps to embellish bookmarks or tabs, and you can even use embossing materials with the stamps you created yourself!

Printing on Fabric

Printing on fabric is so much fun and definitely possible even with our tiny, delicate carvings. Be sure to select smooth fabrics if you have fine details you want to print clearly. Highly textured fabric, such as denim, will require a printing ink to print clearly, which will work best with bold designs. Remember that thick inks you apply with a brayer will fill your minuscule details upon application. You can also print with inks on fabric, depending on the item on which you are printing. I have used black archival ink to print on fabric, which I would set with a hot iron, followed by a hot wash. The ink lightens slightly in the wash, but when set with heat, it sticks around. I printed stamps onto a thin gauze that I then sold as baby swaddling blankets! I have also received a gift from an eraser carver that was her eraser stamp printed on silk and embroidered into earrings. If you can think it, try it, maybe you're on the edge of creating something awesome.

Stamping into Clay

When I took my first ceramic class I just wanted to play in the mud, and I didn't realize how much you can really do with clay. Manipulating and decorating clay is an entire art form in itself, and when I realized this, the first thing I did was press some of my favorite eraser stamps into a bowl that I made. I figured out the right method and materials to use to make three-dimensional versions of my miniature carvings. Printmaking is not the limit of this art form. I went on to make functional ceramic pieces decorated with my eraser stamps; seeing my tiny prints serving a purpose was really cool.

Making Wax Seals

When my children had a random day off of school, and we headed to the craft store for potion supplies we came home with apothecary bottles with cork stoppers and spent the day mixing colors of mica powder into water with food coloring. We made itty bitty labels to put names on our potions and started sealing the corks with wax. We had spent hours already playing, making a mess, and having fun when I realized that I probably could do something cool that would impress my kids, but I didn't know if it would work. I pulled out my carving supplies and made a round, wax seal stamp. I wondered if the pink rubber would melt into the wax and become tacky, but it stamped and worked perfectly!

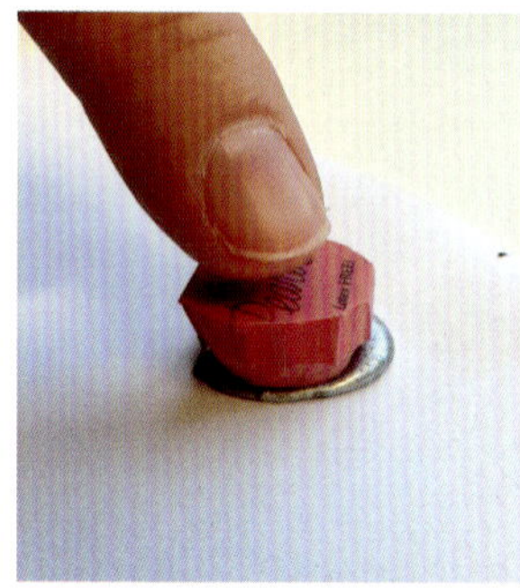

Tips for carving wax seals: take note that when you press the stamp into the wax, the wax will fill your negative space areas and will immortalize all of your carving lines into the raised parts of the wax seal. My most successful wax seal was a line drawing, in which I carved out the drawn lines and did not have any wide negative spaces. The wax filled in the tiny carving areas beautifully and made a clean impression.

26

Evolution of the Pink Eraser Art Project

I hope by this point in reading this book you have felt the joy of tapping in to being creative with silly things. I call pink eraser art my silly little art medium for a reason. Maybe some of these lessons have been frustrating or tedious, and maybe you've had to set it down, walk away, and take a breather. That is real. We are learning something new together. But also, I hope you have had moments that spark joy. I hope you stamped a tiny little print and gasped. I hope you've smiled. I hope you've found the courage to try something that felt scary. I hope that from these experiences you are finding your mind wandering into the "what if?" place. I hope, truly, that you have answered that question with something that felt outrageous and a little dumb, and that it made you laugh.

Now, I will take a minute to tell you about something that made me laugh out loud alone in a hotel room. In 2022, I began carving one hundred tiny artworks into erasers, and as I shared this process each day, more and more people joined in to cheer me on. On the last day of the project, I livestreamed as I carved eraser number one hundred, my signature "Cactus Clouds Art," and I asked everyone viewing to shout out where they were watching from. The answers blew me away: "Australia!" "Hello from Brazil!" "France!" "Love from Cairo!" "Hi, from Germany!" "Singapore, here!" And the greetings from artists and viewers across the globe continued to grow, along with the very real feelings of gratitude and amazement I was feeling.

As a celebratory sign-off for the 100 Eraser Project, I was sponsored by my local newspaper, *This Is Tucson,* to take my artwork the opposite direction of tiny and create a pink eraser art mural inside of a hotel room in Tucson's Hotel McCoy. As the date for the Annual Art Fest came around, I spent each day prepping walls, painting a rainbow, being slightly haunted by monsoon ghosts, and loving every second of it.

With my wall prepped and background painted, I stood back and flipped the switch on my vintage schoolroom projector. As the eraser art images appeared on the wall in front of me, it happened. I was struck by the whimsy. And even though I had a deadline, a literal event, where hundreds of people would come to watch me bring the mural to life, I dropped everything and bolted to the craft store for a block of foam and a can of the pinkest paint.

Because I had to create an eraser big enough to "stamp" my artwork on the mural wall. I didn't have a choice. The "What if?" and the call of the whimsy had to be answered. Over the next few hours, I fashioned a massive pink eraser out of a foam block so that I could return to the mural space and film a video pretending to stamp the artwork onto the wall.

MAKE MORE
ART
Pink Eraser Art

Pink Eraser Art

TUCSON
ART
MAKE MORE ART

TUCSON
ART
MAKE MORE ART

It was dumb. I don't even think the video went viral; it didn't make me any money, and absolutely set back my progress on the mural. But the joy that it brought me was real. And worth every penny and moment spent.

Bestie, I hope that creating from this book has taught you to see potential whimsy in everything. A mundane eraser is no longer just a little chunk of thing that lives at the bottom of your desk drawer, but an object of opportunity that can open up a world of joy for you. Do the silly thing. Answer the call when your own creative brain asks, "What if?" You're going to love it.

Notes for Educators

From the first week of sharing my eraser art with the world online my inbox has been full of the same question, "Can I please use this idea in my classroom?" And every single time I have responded "Yes!"

I have always been passionate about inspiring youth with creative ideas, and I am thrilled every time I receive a photograph of eraser prints from a classroom group! I have received messages from community groups, nonprofits, libraries, and art teachers with these artistic group photos and I love it.

So, before I go on any further: yes, share this with your classroom. Tell your local library activities committee about it. Bring this book into your classroom. Lend it out to your teacher friends and coworkers. I have tried my best to fill this book with the answers to every question a student could ask during the carving process so that you can use this as a complete guide to teach and share and uplift students and community members alike.

Story time: After teaching eraser carving on Instagram live for a few months, I returned to my high school to teach their art classes the craft. I was an OG alum, "famous" on Instagram and viral on TikTok so I was already cool, especially when I let them wave at my followers through an IG video. And then I handed all of these teenagers knives. Some were nervous, others were all too eager to use those blades. And everyone made amazing art.

The thing about printmaking is that even if your drawing isn't perfect, there is still a very cool, grungy, punk rock vibe about it. And even when a student doesn't feel confident about what they have carved, as soon as it has been inked and stamped, it is just cool. Even if you feel like your carving is lacking, if you print it well, it has a vibe and it sparks something inside you.

I went on to teach several art classes that day, and at one point, we drew up short on the tool count. While the art teacher and admin looked around the classroom, I left through the library to find a restroom, and I discovered the most amazing thing. The art students had snuck off to the library with those missing blades. They stole the knives! And then distributed them to their friends, with a pilfered box of erasers and were teaching their friends how to carve erasers as well.

Those students spent their class time learning this art form and immediately turned into teachers themselves. Their parting thought as they left my lesson was the need to share the craft with other people. That is humanity. That is what makes art astounding.

So, please. Share this art form. Let's make art accessible and light that spark of creativity in our communities.

Note: When purchasing supplies for your classroom, be sure to purchase blade sets that have those minuscule V-shaped blades. Not all sets come with the same blade collection, and you want to be sure to set your classroom up for success.

Final Thoughts

When I was a little kid, I had two dreams: I wanted to photograph wildlife for *National Geographic,* and I wanted to publish a book. I studied photography but set the dream aside when I decided to start a family. I keep up wildlife photography as a hobby by photographing my kids in their natural habitat and using my phone's 15x zoom like a nerd to identify birds. My obsessive need to photograph vultures still lives inside me, and will be realized when it is time, and that's just fine with me because right now I get to work on the second dream.

I always considered myself a story author and wrote an entire book in sixth grade. In high school, I started working with a local jeweler, Piney Hollow, who allowed me to take over her work teaching children how to bead. I got a job with the city of Tucson Parks & Recreation teaching children beading and juggling. (I can't believe the ADHD was not evident at that point.) It brought me so much joy to guide children through creating something of which they could be proud. In high school, I worked with my class to plan an activities tour through the Arizona Sonoran Desert Museum for fourth graders, and I loved it. I started volunteering at Rocks & Ropes, teaching children how to climb rock walls every Saturday morning. Cheering those kids on as they conquered their fears was the coolest. After quitting my internship writing for a local newspaper, I went to college for writing. It never occurred to me that maybe teaching is what I should have been looking at instead.

It wasn't until years later, when I was establishing myself as an artist, that I began teaching again. I taught watercolor painting to adults, which became my favorite thing. Helping adults reconnect with their creativity sustained me in the best way. My full income came from teaching workshops in venues across my city, until April of 2020, when everything in our lives was put on pause due to COVID-19. My career as an artist changed, and I focused on my own skills more than introducing new skills to others. In 2022, with not an extra penny to my name, I started sharing my eraser carvings on social media. After so many inquiries to learn, I began teaching again through Instagram livestreaming.

All of that is to say, it isn't a surprise to me that my first book is not a novel, but a lesson. That instead of weaving a plot of mystery and intrigue, I am writing a book of instructions and guidance to activate your mind and body in creative ways; a book of permission to do something silly, for no reason other than that it brings you joy.

I hope you have enjoyed this book. I hope you are really proud of what you've created. I hope you have had some of those creative juices flowing in new ways. I hope you notice things you didn't notice before, and that you are seeing the world with new eyes, because that is what happens when we create. We are pulled into the present, made more aware, and feel more alive and alert. I have done my best to give you the tools to access your creativity, and now I urge you to continue creating with your own. May you reach the point that your own abilities begin to inspire your creativity.

Thanks for being here with me. I appreciate you.

<3 Serena

Global Gallery: Eraser Art from Around the World

From the first day that I started this silly little art medium it has been the enthusiasm of my followers and creatives around the glove that have made pink eraser art what it is. It is the people who dove in headfirst when I hosted the first 30-day challenge, the ones who have filled my inbox with photos of their own artwork, and the teachers around the world sharing this art form with upcoming generations that bring the magic. Pink eraser art wouldn't be what it is without your enthusiasm and joy and support. And so, I am excited to share this gallery of pink eraser art from around the world. Please share yours as well!

Instagram: @pinkeraserart
@cactuscloudsart

TikTok: @cactuscloudsart

Facebook: facebook.com/cactuscloudsart

YouTube: youtube.com/@Cactuscloudsart

"Can't Be Erased" by Casey Wang, Florida, USA. IG: @Pkmn_professor_case

"Alter Egos" by Lisa Menou, New York, USA. @luluvision

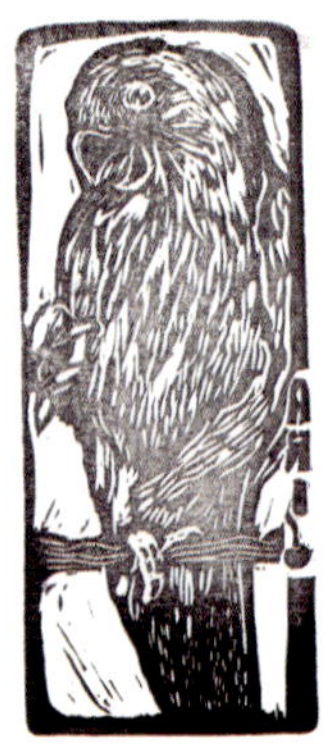

"Chicken" by Ariana Crockett, Arizona, USA. @aricherryart

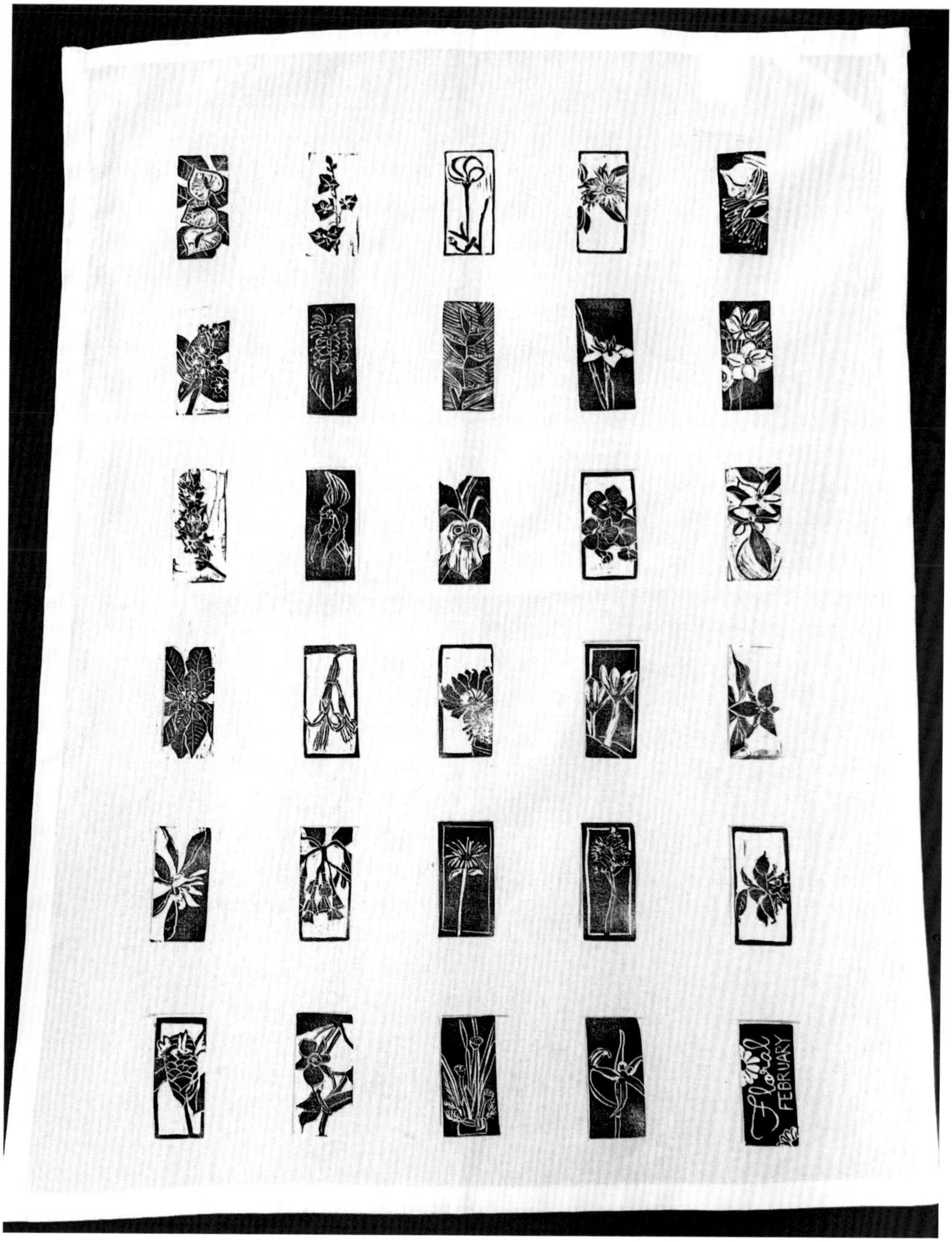

"February Floral Alphabet Tea Towel" by Kirsty Leishman, Queensland, Australia. @leishmankirsty

"Lemon Season" by Coretta Loughmiller, Florida, USA. @corettadeesign

“Les 100 Gommes” by Delphine Bucher, Montbeliard, France.
@dernierechanceeditions

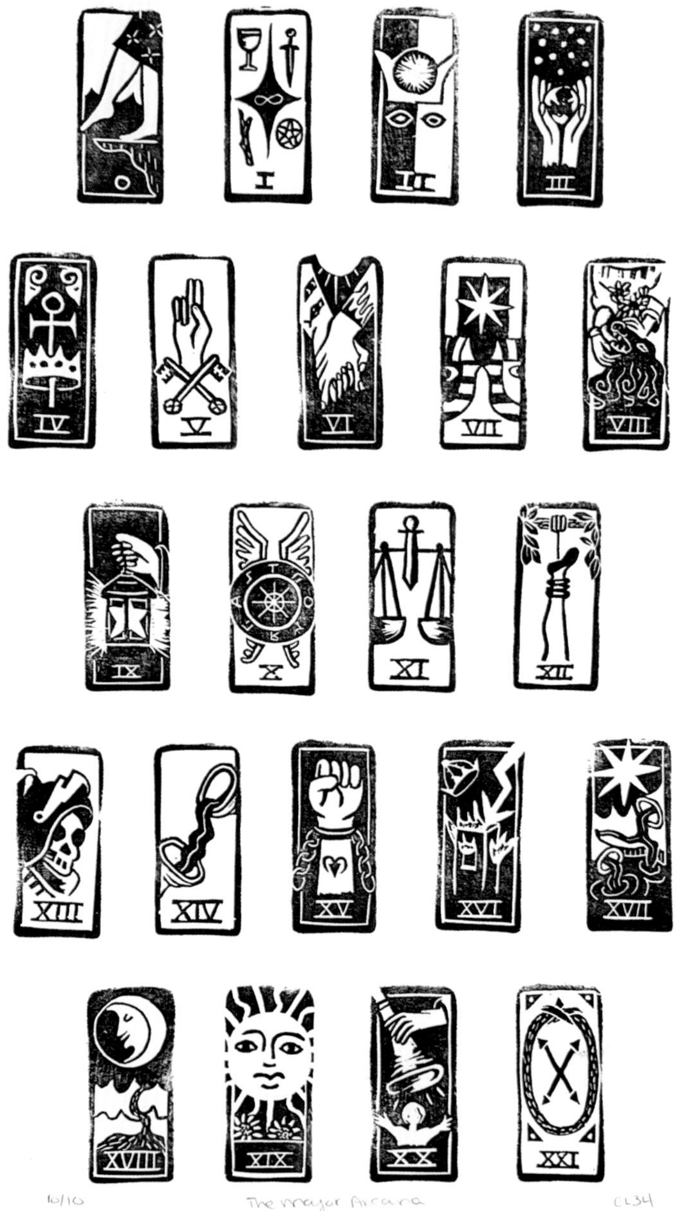

“Major Arcana” by Caitlyn Frances, California, USA.
@art.caitlynfrances

"Pink Eraser Artober Challenge 2023" by CherylAnn Meredith, Ohio, USA.
@worksbycherylann

"The Public Labyrinth" by Engel.

Acknowledgements

First, and before everything else, thank you to my husband, Michael, for standing beside me through the ugly, traumatizing thing that has been my mental health journey. Thank you for keeping us all fed, alive, and well. You are the literal best and my BFF for life. To Juliet and Amelia, you blow me away every day with your creative genius, and I am endlessly inspired by you. It is the honor of my life to raise you. Ari, thank you for getting me out of the house and for being there when I need a friend on the good days and the mentally difficult ones. You are the friend I've been searching for. To Maggie, thank you for helping me heal. In fact, I think I have a good portion of the good things in my life for which to thank you.

To my editor Kelly, thank you for sending me the greatest email of 2024, and one of the greatest emails of my life. To the team at Rocky Nook, thank you for believing in me and helping make a dream into a reality. To the folks at Scented Leaf, thank you for creating the most beautiful out-of-office office, and for fueling the writing of this book with the best drinks a girl could ask for. I do my best work while sipping mango glitter. To Gloria and Elvia, at This Is Tucson, thank you for always cheering me on and supporting my latest projects in the best ways. To Honey, thank you for always being ready and willing to document my favorite projects with your glorious photography skills. You are magic. And to Hotel McCoy, for being ready for me incoming with any new creative endeavor, ready to offer a wall or a workshop space. You have honored me and my work, and I am endlessly grateful.

To my Instagram subscribers, you are the OGs. Thank you for helping me learn how to teach the concept of this silly little art medium. Because of your willingness to spend time on my live streams, asking me questions and making requests, I gained the experience I needed to be able to write this book. To my subscribers on Patreon, you have filled me with confidence through this entire process. Thank you for your feedback and insights as I wrote this book, your kind messages, always cheering me on, and for just being an uplifting bunch in general. You rock. And to my followers across Instagram, Facebook, TikTok, Threads, and YouTube: THANK YOU for bringing your enthusiasm into my life. I get to do what I do because of YOU. No art project has ever gone viral without the enthusiasm of real human beings. Thank you for every comment, and every time you shared my silly little art videos with your friends and loved ones. You are the reason I get to do this.

And finally, to Tucson. Tucson, you perfect city full to the brim of the most genuine, loving family of artists and art lovers. You have fueled everything that I do with your kindness, enthusiasm, and love. Thank you to everyone who has introduced themselves at markets or while I was live painting a mural. Thank you to every parent who has brought your children to my events to show me their precious sketchbooks. Thank you to everyone who has ever attended one of my workshops; everyone who has arrived, sweaty and panting, to be the first at my market booth; and to everyone who is wearing a piece of my apparel, or has my art displayed in your home. It is an honor to be part of this community.

With the biggest, mushiest feelings, thank you!

About the Author

Serena Rios McRae is a Tucson, Arizona, native who is obsessed with the fine details of nature, prismatic color, and local food. She finds humans to be absolutely delightful and loves encouraging creativity in others.

Serena is a working artist, mother, and mental health advocate. She speaks openly about her experiences with postpartum depression, bipolar disorder, and ADHD, working to break stigmas around mental illness and encouraging humans to get the help they need without shame.

Serena follows her ADHD impulses to learn many mediums to create art in often unusual forms: watercolor paintings on animal skulls, murals on taco trucks, intricate relief carvings on tiny pink erasers, as well as clay and classic watercolor on paper. She is the creator of Affirmations Moms Actually Need (funded 173% on Kickstarter) and the Pink Eraser Art Project. Serena posts on social media as Cactus Clouds Art. As she creates, Serena encourages others to discover their creativity as well with tutorials and lessons. As much of her work is built from her experiences with mental illness, she strives to help others also find healing in art.

@cactuscloudsart

@pinkeraserart